HAUNTED
COVENTRY

HAUNTED
COVENTRY

DAVID McGRORY

In memory of Vic Tandy, the man who tried to explain the unexplained.

Frontispiece: *Lychgate Cottages in Priory Row photographed from Holy Trinity churchyard.*

First published in 2005 by Tempus Publishing
Reprinted 2007

Reprinted in 2009 by
The History Press
The Mill, Brimscombe Port,
Stroud, Gloucestershire, GL5 2QG
www.thehistorypress.co.uk

Reprinted 2013

British Library Cataloguing in Publication Data.
A catalogue record for this book is available from the British Library.

ISBN 978 0 7524 3708 8

Typesetting and origination by
Tempus Publishing Limited.
Printed in Great Britain.

CONTENTS

ACKNOWLEDGEMENTS

Many thanks to the following for supplying information: Peter Walters, Vic Tandy, John Ashby, Richard Hoare, Dave Nightingale, June Whitfield, Tony Rose, *Coventry Evening Telegraph*, June Fairbrother, Coventry City Libraries – Local Studies, Jean Field, David Stringer, Paul Stringer, David Betts, Sue and Ron Freemantle, S. King, Amanda Higginson, Steve Ball, Maurice Burnell, Tom Reale, Mrs Merchant, Pat Wightman, Rob Orland, John Stanton, David Monks, Roger Symonds, Ron Severs, Valerie Frame, Steve Bagley, Steve Ball and Carol Cowley.

Also, thanks for photographs to: *Coventry Evening Telegraph*, Coventry City Libraries – Local Studies, CVOne, Chris Barnes, Maurice Burnell, Haddon Davies, David Monks, Tony Rose and Roger Symonds. All other illustrations are from the David McGrory Collection.

'Science and the Cellar' is based on Vic Tandy's paper entitled 'Something in the Cellar'. 'The Earlsdon Ghost' – originally 'The Watchmaker's Widow' – was first published in the *Echo* in March 2005.

INTRODUCTION

In the Rolls of the Warwickshire and Coventry Sessions of Peace from 1377-97 one entry records that John Herthull is *mortuus est*, dead, and that not only is he dead but we are told he also walks by night. It would be tempting to say that Herthull was Coventry's oldest known ghost to walk the streets but sadly it more than likely means that John Herthull himself may have died before his case came up or was not actually dead but was alive and wandering the streets in the dead of night, beyond curfew, when all the good people of Coventry were abed. John Herthull, not his ghost, was probably fined for his misdemeanour.

That said, Coventry and its districts do boast some real ghosts, coming to us in all shapes and sizes, misty or solid, black or white or even grey. Sadly, practically no supernatural tales have survived from ancient Coventry, which was surely awash with spectres. Likewise few pre-war ghost stories survive. Most of the sources I have checked have lost such records or they have mysteriously disappeared, like the spectres we are seeking.

The odd thing about writing about ghosts is that people either believe or don't believe – some would be sceptical until an actual encounter, and even then they might still doubt. It seems, however, that the many people do believe and have either had experiences or know someone else who has. Unfortunately, not everyone wants to share their experiences, resulting in a deficit of actual recorded sightings. This was probably also the case in the past, when only the brave would state in the press that they had actually seen a ghost.

Coventry had its own notable 'ghost hunter', Vic Tandy. Vic was based at Coventry University and experimented with low-frequency sounds. Vic had identified these sounds in some places that had claimed to be haunted. He first came upon this theory when he and others were working in a laboratory and they kept getting the strange feeling that they were not alone. He investigated and found that a fan in the lab was giving off low-frequency vibrations. Vic believed the 'haunting' coincided with the fan running, which was responsible for the strange feelings he and others were experiencing.

Vic believed that low-frequency infrasound at certain levels may create the phenomena that are ghosts. That said, he could not deny that low frequency may not be the creator but may enable the phenomena to come through more easily or help people to better perceive it. Vic was a scientist, but of the best kind – he still kept an open mind.

A photograph of an unexplained presence at an incident taken somewhere in Coventry in the 1980s. (David Monks)

Whatever scientists may think, they still cannot explain why people see ghosts, not only of people but of animals and vehicles. Low frequency may give you a 'funny feeling' but it cannot explain why a horse-drawn carriage hurtles up the Tamworth Road in the dead of night, or why a highwayman waits at the roadside in Westwood Heath in the late twentieth century.

Coventry is and has always been haunted and within these pages you will find phantom monks, grey ladies, the devil himself, rattling chains, a ghost that appears to do the washing up and a phantom lorry. Just a taste of the many spirits in haunted Coventry, old and new.

ONE

THE CITY CENTRE

The ghosts of St Mary's Hall

St Mary's Hall in Bayley Lane dates from 1342 and is considered one of the finest guildhalls in England. The hall was built by the rich merchant guild of St Mary, which amalgamated with three other guilds to become the guild of the Holy Trinity. The hall has welcomed kings and queens, including Henry V, Henry VI and James II to name but a few. Other famous individuals to visit the hall include William Shakespeare, George Eliot and Charles Dickens.

The hall also has other visitors who are sometimes heard but rarely seen; these include a grey lady, a woman in black and a man wearing a medieval skullcap. The Grey Lady has been seen going down the stairs into the medieval kitchen and turning under the stairs. The kitchen also has other visitors; an electrician working there some years ago saw a man standing near the entrance to the undercroft who faded away before his eyes. He was so shocked by the sight that he refused to return to the hall.

Another incident happened a few years ago. Valerie Frame, who then worked as a cook in the kitchen, came in one morning and saw a woman dressed in black who appeared to be washing something in the sink. She said hello, put her coat in the staffroom and was then asked by another member of staff who she was talking to. Valerie told her what she had seen only to discover that no-one else was there. She did however catch a glimpse of the lady in black again, standing at the bottom of the stairs which lead into the Great Hall.

These stairs occasionally surprise others, including the Senior Heritage Assistant of the hall who one Sunday morning distinctly heard someone running up the stairs behind him. Nobody was there. Later on two occasions the heavy wooden doors at the top of the stairs opened on their own. This was witnessed by the two guides; the senior guide, putting his hand around the door as it was opening, noted that it was actually opening against a draught.

The old Council Chamber, which was the meeting place of the inner circle of the council and the guild, is a room of great antiquity and beauty. In it sits one of the rarest state chairs in England, which originated from Coventry Priory. Here, it is said, has occasionally been glimpsed a man in red, scarlet being the colour worn by members of the Trinity Guild. For one day only, in 2001, the room suffered from not a cold spot, but a smell spot, for in one place and one place only was the strong smell of violets, which lasted all day. More recently the floorboards creaked loudly as they do on entering the chamber and somebody was heard clearly to sit on the eighteenth-century bench, which creaked under their weight. However, at the time no-one was in the room! Beyond the Council Chamber is the Treasury, where some have claimed a 'feeling' and shadows have been seen moving across the floor.

The Prince's Chamber is another fine room, panelled with Jacobean oak and containing a huge fire surround. This room is largely untroubled by paranormal phenomena, except for two occasions in 2002 when a large pool of blood appeared by the entrance. When the blood was studied it was found to be semi-transparent and brown, yet when it was lying upon the oak boards it appeared very red. On both occasions the 'blood' quickly disappeared, leaving not the slightest trace of its presence.

The Great Hall has been the meeting place of the guild and council for centuries; monarchs have dined here, plays have been performed here and criminals sentenced to death and transportation within its walls. During a banquet in the Great Hall on 22 January 1985 a photograph was taken in which many claim stands a strange figure resembling a monk at the back of the dais. Those who have seen the photograph afterwards claim the figure was not there when it was actually taken and there were certainly no monks present at the banquet. To me the figure bears more of a resemblance to a gorilla in a monk's habit. This photograph has become quite famous and has appeared in many books on the paranormal and on the television. What it shows may not be a ghost but could be two people standing close together; the angle further confuses the image. That said, some parts of the image are strangely unaccountable and this area of the dais isn't a stranger to unusual events. During a recent banquet a seated woman heard disembodied footsteps mount the dais and something unseen brushed past her as she sat at her meal. Not surprisingly the lady in question fled the building. Also of interest, but not usually pointed out, are the three figures at the other end of the table who appear to be monks with their cowls up.

To the right of the dais is the room in which Mary Queen of Scots was accommodated during her short stay in the building. One version of the City Annals places the Scottish Queen here in the Old Mayoress's Parlour just at the close of November 1569. Mary is reputed to haunt dozens of places, though not here. There is, however, something in this room, which once housed a chamber of horrors: wax heads of guillotined aristocracy belonging to the real Madame Tussaud in the eighteenth century. Moreover, nine years ago one of the hall's guides recalls one Sunday when someone appeared to be throwing furniture around in the room. Each time he opened the doors the sound immediately stopped. This happened on three occasions. Later that year both of these heavy decorated oak doors were apparently seen on a number of occasions to be swung open by some unseen hands.

Carol Cowley attended a seminar in this room – one she won't quickly forget. As she sat at her table writing with a pencil she felt something touch her; the touch turned into a cold shiver which ran down her arm. She then noticed that the pencil she was holding appeared to have turned to rubber and wobbled in her hand. Suddenly, with the chink of breaking ice, the pencil snapped cleanly in half, with no splinters as would be normal from such a breakage.

If this was not enough, Carol then began to notice the face of the tutor as she sat by the window. Shadows were crossing her face, like clouds moving across a hillside and gradually her feminine features slowly began to alter to that of a bearded man wearing a black skullcap. Carol at this point had to leave the room, and when she returned all was well. The bearded man may still wander the hall and could have been the one seen in the kitchen by the electrician.

Another encounter occurred in the Minstrel's Gallery. Guides stood and watched as an unknown presence walked along the creaking floorboards of the Minstrel's Gallery. The senior

Opposite: *The well-known ghost photograph taken during a banquet in the hall in 1985. (Haddon Davies)*

Right: *A close-up of the photograph opposite, showing the unusual figure in the corner.*

guide actually saw a brocaded dress or gown sweep past him as he climbed the spiral staircase onto the gallery. This was so clear he was able to identify the pattern as fifteenth century. Members of the catering staff have also heard footsteps coming down the stairs, disconcertingly with no-one attached.

Sometimes things move, as the catering staff found when unseen hands moved decorative ribbon from one table to another. Sound systems have volumes turned up and down, or switch themselves on. Lights are switched on, and monies moved. It has even been claimed that the heavy oak second door into the armoury was once lifted off its hinges and moved across the room. Outside the room a heavy Victorian coathanger occasionally moves itself, blocking the entrance to the ladies' toilet.

Why these phenomena occur in the hall, and who these ghosts are, one can only speculate. The lady in black in the kitchen may be an old kitchen hand from Victorian times. The man in the skullcap could be anyone from the medieval period who may have passed away in the building, perhaps a hall keeper. As for the Grey Lady, she is a classic English ghost who can be found throughout this land.

On 22 January 2005 the Midlands Ghost Research Society held a vigil in the hall, bristling with equipment to detect changes in temperature, magnetic fluctuations, etc. They produced a thirty-nine-page report on the hall which recorded variable results. One of the first unusual things they mention took place in the Treasury, where someone said they felt something had touched them and there was a smell of perfume. Another member of the team thought they had seen a mist move over the table and noises outside the door were reported. It was also reported that the doors of the seventeenth-century cupboard opened 'loudly' on their own. 'Orbs' were also seen and photographed. These balls of light, which are said to be often seen in haunted buildings, may simply be the reflection of light off dust particles, but possibly have a more spectral origin.

The south end of the Great Hall, the Minstrel's Gallery and the four doorways downstairs which lead to rooms which have experienced ghostly happenings.

The old Council Chamber off the Great Hall.

Orbs were also reported as moving around in the Great Hall and at the same time fluctuations were recorded in the electromagnetic fields. Kevin Wallace reported that he and another investigator 'both witnessed a small ball of light appear in the far right corner of the Great Hall (looking at the stage) and travel up the wall ... the light was quite bright...' A smell of perfume was also perceived as it has done in the past in the old Council Chamber. Another member, Jim Garrett, reported that he twice heard a high-pitched woman's voice whisper near the dais, 'Look left', but on looking all that could be seen was another researcher. On the dais itself a 'strange blurring light' was picked up by a digital camera. At the same time an orb was seen to climb up the wall and the electromagnetic fields fluctuated.

In the so-called 'Mary Queen of Scots Room' (she was really held in the bottom of the hall in the Old Mayoress's Parlour) bangs were heard and some researchers suffered equipment failure, including drained batteries. The report states that some thought the room was getting colder despite the fact that the thermometer was going up.

The group reported that the Ante Room upstairs was the most active, saying that many felt a change as they entered the room and many felt sick. One fully charged camcorder battery went dead upon entering the room. Significantly nine people reported hearing footsteps either going up or down the newel staircase and shuffling outside the door. Other reported events included the feeling of something blowing on the neck, the door shutting on its own, orbs, light flashes and temperature fluctuations.

The hall continues to intrigue with its marvellous history and the occasional sound or sighting.

Left: *The ruins of St Mary's Priory, near the alleged tunnel.*

Below: *Thomas Chapman, the man who chased the ghost from Lychgate Cottage.*

Ghosts of Priory Row

The late Abe Jephcott recorded in his notes written in the 1940s two ghost stories concerning Priory Row. In his handwritten notes he recorded:

When a site for the girl's Blue Coat School was being prepared a flight of eleven stone steps was uncovered about 8ft down. These led to a vault in a crypt which had been hidden for 300 years. It had two stone doorways and these can be seen today... Before they were bricked up a few ghostly stories about an underground passage from here to Kenilworth began to float and settle in the priory ruins.

Here we have no story like the curse of the creeping monk, but we have others, just as good! It was midnight when a man accompanied by his dog started out to explore the tunnel ... the tunnel was of course a haunted one ... they say the dog returned, but the man was never seen again!

The next story is a little heavy, but it persists even today. In one of the half-timbered houses built on the priory foundations there was a clumsy poltergeist ghost that upset every room. He opened windows and shut doors with a bang. At night he banged doors and clumped about the room as if he was wearing heavy boots across the creaking oak floors. He was eventually chased out by a well-known Coventrian, Mr ——, who chased him with an old weapon shouting, 'Where the hell are you?' The poor ghost must have been frightened to death as he stumbled back into the priory ruins.

The cottage in question was No. 4 Priory Row. Thomas Chapman was the well-known Coventry character who lived here. He was a watchmaker by trade and also a bit of a thespian, not adverse to playing Hamlet with a skull he kept in the cottage. Thomas also collected antique weapons and his cottage was full of swords, knives and guns. It was probably with one of his old swords that Thomas chased the poltergeist from his cosy timbered cottage in Priory Row.

The phantom monk, Priory Row

Coventry's great priory church of St Mary was dissolved by Henry VIII in 1539 and sold on in 1545 to speculators John Combe and Richard Stansfield, who afterwards sold it on to John Hales. These men had the once grand building stripped from roof to base, selling the stone by the yard. The once beautiful priory church was turned into a veritable builders' yard and soon nothing but part of the west entrance remained. It was said at the time that the Benedictine monks of Coventry Priory were glad to leave the priory for they were already semi-destitute. In the mid-nineteenth century a large bunch of medieval keys were found in the River Sherbourne in Palmer Lane, big enough to have belonged to the priory, so it was believed the last monk to leave threw them into the river in disgust.

Not all the monks seem to have left, however, for ghostly monks have been seen around the site of the old priory. In 1955 Mrs Davidson, wife of then retired Dr Davidson, formerly of 15 Priory Row, wrote to the *Coventry Standard* about one ghostly monk who shared their house:

A photograph taken by Roger Symonds in December 2003 shows a strange mist and what appears to be one or two figures in Coventry's original cathedral's undercroft. Roger said of this picture, 'I took it at lunchtime; all the before and after pictures were clear and all were taken within fifteen minutes.'

In 1879 the late Dr Davidson left the Navy and started a practice there [No. 15]. Previously it had belonged to Dr Anderson who lived and practised there until he retired and left for London. During our residence 'the Grey Monk' was seen by all my family, my husband, myself and several maids. I asked Miss Helen Rotherham, who was a childhood friend and contemporary of Miss Anderson, if when she next wrote to Miss Anderson she would casually ask if they had ever thought 15 Priory Row was haunted.

Miss Anderson replied, 'My mother told me that a few days after I was born when my father was out visiting a patient, she awakened to see a grey monk sitting beside her bed. He asked if he might nurse me, which he did. He blessed me and placed me beside her.

'The next encounter with the monk that I know of was at the end of the First World War. I had guests to dinner that night, amongst whom were the late Mr Dick Rotherham and his young daughter, now Lady Kittermaster, Vicomte de Sarigny and Miss Eardley-Wilmot and two others. We had finished dinner and had gone upstairs to the drawing room when I heard terrible screams coming from the top landing. There I saw my small daughter clad in her nightgown standing in the archway looking very white and scared. She said an old man had tried to lift her out of bed. She refused to go back and as Nurse was helping the maids, I wrapped her in a shawl and took her downstairs. Eventually her bed was taken into my room.

Miss Anderson said that during the following weeks she saw the shadow of the monk walking in front of her on the stairs. She also pointed out that No. 15 was a large and rambling house and they often heard footsteps and creaking sounds but previously had always blamed it on the old oak floorboards.

The house on the right was the haunt of the Grey Monk for years. This is one of the few photographs in existence showing the building before its destruction.

The monk came back, as she recalled: 'My second daughter home for her holiday from Sherbourne School, also had a visit from the grey monk. She was sleeping with her blinds drawn up on a brilliant moonlit night and she awoke to see the monk beside her bed with an old-fashioned candle lantern which he held high up to his chest. His hand was round the glass and his eyes were gazing down at the candle. She declares that had he raised his head, she would have collapsed in fear. However, she pulled on the electric light cord over her bed and he immediately vanished.

'Another evening we had been to dine with Colonel Wyley at the Charterhouse. It was between 11.30 p.m. and midnight and after we returned, my husband sat reading the daily paper in our breakfast room when somebody walked past the door and up the stairs. He asked me why the maids were up so late. However, they were all in bed and we looked around the house and saw no-one.'

'One Christmas night soon after my son had seen the old Monk, I also saw him. We had several house guests and a few people to dinner, including Bishop Mervyn Haigh, then bishop of Coventry and Mr and Mrs Oliver Bellasis. I went upstairs to get some Japanese crackers to amuse the party when the monk came past me. I rushed back and rather breathlessly told the party. They laughed me to scorn.

'I was constantly having maids complaining to me of footsteps outside their door and in fact knocking, not once but twice during the night. Certainly our Monk had a roguish sense of humour. The sensation of some presence in the room or behind my chair was often with me, but it never worried me at all.'

She recalls a visitor's sightings, 'We had some friends staying with us for the Warwickshire Hunt Ball … amongst them being a stockbroker from London, Gilbert Williamson … I remember we were all thrilled because he arrived in a super car… Gilbert was put in the Yellow Room where several times the ghost had walked, but I never gave it a thought. Apparently his whole night was disturbed. He woke up twice to find his bedroom door wide open, and the third time he turned the latch thinking the lock was broken. But at dawn he was awakened again to see a grey figure walking through the door.

'I did not know of this incident until a year later… The late George Belcher happened to be one of the guests … and they had by mistake put him in the haunted room, and he had a terrifying night. On one occasion we were going for our holidays in Scotland… Our old cook had come to Rugby station with my husband to help us pack into the train. She left the between maid…When they returned the poor girl had locked herself in the kitchen and refused to move. She said she had seen an old man in a grey cloak standing on the stairs, and he "frightened her to death".'

Two months after this appeared in the *Coventry Standard* Mrs Edith Poynton, an ex-maid, contacted the paper to tell of her story. She had had an experience at the beginning of the Second World War and had never mentioned it to Mrs Davidson. She recalled:

The family had gone to Jamaica for a holiday… The house was empty and my duties entailed me going there alone in the evenings. I was a little afraid of being by myself there so my husband would come with me. I was with him in the kitchen one evening when the telephone bell rang in the hall.

The telephone was in a kind of alcove from which one could see across the hall and down a fairly long passage to the dining room. I picked up the receiver and was about to answer. Then I looked casually down the passage towards the dining room door. It was open and standing in front of it, facing me, was a tall figure in the habit of a monk. His habit was of a greyish colour… I dropped the receiver and ran back to my husband. I didn't wait to see what sort of face the monk had or what the expression was in his eyes. He was definitely coming from the dining room … he had his right arm lifted up with the palm of his hand facing me.'

The householder Mrs Davidson concluded:

Eventually I found it was increasingly difficult to keep my staff, and after three maids had complained of being disturbed by the ghost's nocturnal visits, I asked a priest to come and exorcise our poor old Monk. Solemnly the priest, and I, with the three maids … visited every hole and corner of the old house and I think he was well and truly laid, for we never saw him again. I hope he is at rest and happy because he was a quiet and friendly ghost.

The ghostly monk of Priory Row is unusual, for the his witnesses are impeccable with their sightings, ranging from before 1879 until the monk was exorcised after the Second World War. The only outstanding question concerning the monk is why he was wearing a grey habit, as the Benedictines of Coventry Priory were known as the black monks for they wore the black habit! This change in colour may of course be down to the fact that he was a ghost. One high contender for the origins of the ghost is a monk killed a short distance away in the early 1190s. The monks of Coventry were persecuted by monk-hating Bishop Hugh de Nonant. Their hatred of him may have spilled over into attempted murder for, when work was underway on the priory tower which straddled the present Hill Top, someone let drop a large piece of masonry as Nonant was standing underneath. The stone in question just missed the bishop and struck a monk on the head, dashing out his brains. This nameless monk may be our man!

The house our monk so actively haunted was damaged during the war and later demolished during building work on Coventry's new cathedral.

The 'ghosts' of St Michael's

Around 1822 a bricklayer called David Dry, for some strange reason apparent only to himself, decided he wanted to pretend to be a ghost. He went in the early hours of the morning to the north entrance of St Michael's church and there covered himself with a sheet and began to haunt the area. He did this over several nights and by the end of the week the whole of Priory Row had heard or seen the ghost and some had even complained to the magistrate.

An early nineteenth-century engraving of St Michael's. The north door where the monk walked and David Dry haunted can be seen directly under the tower. At the very end of the church (right) can be seen the County Court and Coventry Gaol.

Watchmen were sent there to apprehend the ghost but those who saw it didn't have the nerve except one man named George Farmer, who was described as a 'stout man with a stout heart'. Farmer strode up to the ghost as it glided through the tombstones and stopped it in its tracks, saying, 'Are you a ghost or are you not?' The ghost replied, 'No, Mr Farmer, I am David Dry.' Farmer arrested Dry, white sheet and all and incarcerated him in the watch-house and the next morning the St Michael's 'ghost' received a three-month prison sentence in the local bridewell.

It is interesting that Dry chose the north door of the old cathedral to start his haunts for he would have known the story of the ghostly monk which was said to be seen passing this spot. Its visitations were so regular that a resident in Priory Row was in the habit of taking potshots at it, leaving the north door pocked with musket balls holes. Another story tells of a police officer returning from Draper's Hall and chasing a ghost through the east end of the churchyard.

The church apparently had a history of ghosts inside too. In Sir Herbert Brewer's *Memories of Choirs and Organists* we are informed, 'Owen, who had been a London omnibus conductor, but was then the verger of St Michael's told him of the ghost in 1892, and related how a grey figure appeared and disappeared, how the chief choir boys hurried from the church because of it, how some of the men fell down in sheer fright, how he saw it in one place and then in another, how he chased it to what appeared to be its lair and how it was never found.'

In 1929 'Mercian' wrote in the *Radio Times*:

There is an interesting story connected with St Michael's Church, the truth of which I can vouch for. As far as I know it has never appeared in print, but many of the older Coventry residents may have heard of the incident. One winter's night somewhere, about 1892, my father, who was on a visit to Coventry, was practising on the organ of St Michael's, as it was known in those days, after the church was closed.

The whole building was in darkness with the exception of the lights over the organ. Presently there was a rattle of keys, a door clanged, and the verger, a very matter-of-fact man – he had been a conductor in London in his younger days – entered and made his way to the organ. 'Excuse me sir,' he said, 'but aren't you afraid to be in here alone?' 'No', said my father... 'Then you haven't heard what happened last Friday night?' said the verger; and told the following story.

A churchwarden had died the previous week, and on the night before the funeral the choir were rehearsing the music for the funeral service. On that occasion, also, the building was in darkness, the only lights being those in the choir stalls. Suddenly the verger's son, who was one of the choirboys, cried out, 'Look, father! What's this thing coming up the church?' The singing stopped, and they all saw a grey figure carrying a light, pass slowly up the centre aisle and into the pew usually occupied by the deceased churchwarden. The boys were terrified and ran out of the church, but the men, thinking it might be a practical joker, rushed down the aisle to catch him.

As they approached the pew they saw the light again pass across the west end of the church and disappear behind a wooden hoarding concealing the bells, which at that time were on the floor of the church for restoration. The verger took a flying leap over the barricade, and searched amongst the debris at the back without success. The ghost had vanished. No explanation was ever found for this mystery, although experiments were made with lights both inside and outside the church.

The inside of St Michael's, where a ghost was seen passing up the centre aisle.

This wasn't the first time the story had actually appeared in print, for it first made the news in the *Coventry Herald* on 20 January 1893. The *Herald* told the story much as 'Mercian' had, saying that one of the verger's sons who was standing next to the stove saw in the darkness of the north aisle heading towards the chancel an arm gliding along carrying a 'bluish torch-like light'. The rest confirms 'Mercian' except the choirboys panic and the ghost itself which wasn't a figure but an arm carrying a torch. The following day the *Coventry Standard* also reported the event confirming this saying that:

> At a few minutes to ten o'clock on Friday night, the choir were practising funeral hymns …
> in memoriam of the late Alderman Dalton [churchwarden]. 'Blessed are the Dead' was being
> sung, and the verger was at the west end of the church. Suddenly his attention was called to an

object described as an arm holding aloft 'a torch of bright blue flame'. The object started from the north aisle. It proceeded down the aisle till Mr Dalton's former pew was reached. Then it disappeared, and Owen's [Tom Owen, junior verger] searchings were in vain.

But a few minutes later he asked a choirman if he had seen the light, and immediately the choirman testifies 'it' again appeared at the spot where Owen saw it disappear the first time, and went along the church to the south-west corner, among the bells, etc. that lie there. The verger went to the spot, but to no purpose. This is the man's story – believe it who like… With it is told another; that a horse in one of the funeral carriages on Saturday stopped dead in Hertford Street, at the exact spot where Mr Dalton first felt his indisposition on Christmas evening, and the animal refused to further go.

The same newspaper put forward a probable explanation for the event, saying that when the church had been restored two large coke heating stoves were put inside. Apparently if the doors of the stoves were left open a blue glow would be emitted. It was suggested that if you stood in the right place and noticed this glow then quickly turned towards the other fire 'as if in fright' you could see the blue glow there and this may explain the event. This would only of course work if both stoves were open but we ignore the fact that a number of people saw the 'thing' moving down the church aisle. The interior of the cathedral was burnt out on 14 November 1940, which may or may not have stopped the haunting, assuming of course that it was haunted in the first place.

Science and the cellar, Bayley Lane

Vic Tandy worked for the School of International Studies and Law at Coventry University. As mentioned in the introduction Vic had a theory that when infrasound (sound of a pitch below that audible by the human ear) reaches certain levels it can cause people to hallucinate and experience apparitions. Vic first experienced this in his laboratory when several people claimed to have experienced some strange feelings. Vic believed this experience was caused by a fan giving off a low-frequency sound of 18.9Hz.

Vic first got to test his theory in the field in a cellar in Bayley Lane. This cellar originally belonged under 38/39 Bayley Lane, which was destroyed in the Blitz and lay undiscovered until stumbled across while digging foundations for the Tourist Information Centre, which has since been demolished.

Vic reported that a number of people claimed to have had experiences while in the cellar, many of which were vague, such as a 'funny feeling'. In 1997 Green Badge city guide Colin Cook visited the cellar with a Canadian journalist who, as he entered, experienced a 'funny feeling'. Colin said, 'The gentleman was frozen to the spot and the colour drained from his face, the hairs on his arms rose up and goose-pimples formed.' Soon after, the journalist described the feeling that overtook him as being like, 'a balloon was being pushed between his shoulder blades and an intense feeling of presence'. Eventually he reported that the face of a woman seemed to be peering over his right shoulder.

Greatly concerned as the man grew more disorientated and pale, Colin helped him back upstairs into the Information Centre where he gradually recovered and recounted his tale. On another occasion Colin was again guiding when a Latvian gentleman said he felt a presence, a cold chill and thought there was a ghost in the cellar. On yet another visit Colin was with an

A haunted fourteenth-century cellar still exists below the house in the centre, which was destroyed in the war. The Draper's Hall on the right is mentioned in the text when a policeman left here and pursued a ghost in St Michael's churchyard.

American couple when the woman stopped dead just before entering and claimed to feel a presence which was blocking her way. As she grew paler her husband, who felt nothing, tried to encourage her to enter but she refused.

Vic Tandy stated that, 'Staff at the Information Centre were interviewed and confirmed that a significant number of visitors do report a presence in the cellar but generally give few details.' These included two white witches who claimed the cellar contained the spirit of a woman who was 'friendly'. Another witch disagreed and fled the cellar in terror.

Vic also talked to a Mrs Jung, who took a number of visitors into the cellar and claimed herself to feel the presence, as if she were intruding. This was also mentioned by some German visitors she took in.

The day came when Vic Tandy, Sam Maunder and Bill Dunn descended the two flights of stairs down into the small medieval cellar armed with a Bruel and Kjaer precision sound level meter capable of picking up frequencies down to 1Hz and a Zonic AND-type 3525 Dual Channel FFT analyser. The microphone was placed in the centre of the cellar and was connected to the analyser placed in the entrance. The team left the cellar while the equipment monitored any ambient sound. Low-frequency infrasound was monitored from almost zero and did at one time peak at 19 Hz, the level which Vic had predicted would cause the ghost effect. Tests were made for ambient sounds and Vic sought to trace the source of the 19Hz. His best guess was that the low-frequency sounds were generated by the void at the entrance to the cellar which he believed, because of its shape, would resonate at 18 or 19Hz. The fact that many feelings had been felt at the threshold of this entrance is consistent with Vic's explanation.

Vic pointed out though that 'there is no absolute proof that it was there at all at the time. However, the fact that the corridor has the correct physical proportions to resonate at 19Hz combined with the fact that the experimenters measured it doing so, consistently for several hours, seems sufficient circumstantial evidence to pursue. If the signal were present at around 38dB, it would be completely inaudible.' He added, 'The experiments described found that a frequency of 12Hz … could cause "sudden and violent nausea". It may not surprise you to know that some nations are currently experimenting with infrasound in the hope to use it as a stealth weapon.'

As infrasound can travel over great distances, Vic concluded that the source of energy which created the standing wave in the cellar is still a mystery. He believed that the corridor which leads down into it conducts the sounds which may emanate from elsewhere – where, that's another mystery!

The haunted history of Whitefriars

The friary of the White Friars now stands by the ring-road near to the London Road. It originally stood just within the city wall and housed the friary and church of the Whitefriars (or Carmelites). The friary was founded around 1343 with the help of Sir John Poultney and was dedicated to the Virgin Mary, in honour of whom the monks wore white. This popular but poor order of monks was dissolved in 1538 and left without pensions, as Henry believed that they were so used to begging they could continue in that way. The church quickly disappeared and all that survives is the main cloisters. The building, like most other monastic buildings in the city, then came into the hands of John Hales, baronet and Clerk to the Hanaper. Hales had the remaining building converted into a house and called it 'Hale's Place'. The building remained in the hands of the Hales family for many years and in 1801 the building was purchased by the Guardians of the Poor and turned into a workhouse, which it remained as until 1948.

The building seems to have left some memories behind, one of which dates back to the time of the monks and was still current in 1888. We are told that at the foot of the staircase leading into the cloister was a corbel showing the devil resplendent with horns, thought to have been placed there to commemorate an event which took place in the days of the friars.

It is said that in those times Satan had decided to pay a visit to the devout brothers to see if he could corrupt them. However, on entering the cloister he was immediately perceived by the brothers, who ran at him to cast him out. The Brother Superior, a very large man, got to him first and gave him such a blow that Satan's head was sent cracking against the wall. A dazed Satan pulled himself together just in time and fled the building in shock. Even in the

Left: *Whitefriars in the mid-nineteenth century when it was a workhouse.*

Below: *The cloister in Whitefriars where the devil hit his head. (CVOne)*

Left: *The great room in Whitefriars where Lady Hales' ghost walks. (CVOne)*

Below: *Lady Hales points to the next to die.*

nineteenth century a raised impression on the wall in the cloister was pointed out as the place where Satan banged his head.

When Whitefriars became a workhouse, the timbered hall upstairs, originally the main room of Hales' house, was lined with beds. Whitley records a tale concerning it in 1888: 'There was a story told in a late master and matron's time by an aged inmate as to how at certain times, before an old woman died, Lady Hales' ghost walked through the long room occupied by the aged female inmates in the dread hour of night for three evenings in succession, clothed in white, with her long hair floating over her shoulders, casting sad anxious glances at the inmates on passing them. "I seed it, I seed it," said the old woman, "it walked three times up the room and three times down the room, and then pointed the first skinny finger of its bony right hand towards old Molly, and beckoned towards the cemetery on the road out there, so we knowed she was going to die soon."

The Lady Hales in question is no doubt the one in residence in 1642, who was said to have been killed with her maid by a stray cannonball which struck the tower in Hales' Place when Charles I attacked the city after he was refused permission to bring his entire army inside at the beginning of the Civil War.

As no-one is now in the building at night we cannot say if Lady Hales still walks after her unexpected death. There is however another woman who is still seen. For a number of years archaeologists have used the building and a few years ago one unfortunate connected to them saw the ghost of a woman hanging in a stairwell. He saw her in great detail and claimed that the woman wore Victorian-style boots studded with buttons. The witness to the hanged woman was so convinced that she was real that he was intent upon calling the police. He quickly changed his mind when he returned accompanied to find the hanged woman was gone.

Considering that Whitefriars was a workhouse it is perhaps not surprising that there have been a number of suicides in its history. One such was Margaret Hennessey, who in July 1858 was found hanged in the workhouse after being declared a 'dangerous lunatic' the day before.

Visited by phantom, Gosford Street

As far as I am aware, the oldest ghost story to appear in the local press was in the *Coventry Mercury* on 19 February 1759. The paper records:

> The following occurrence having occasioned much stir in the street where it happened, we shall relate it to our readers.
>
> On Wednesday night last as a Maid Servant to Mr Beas, a baker in Gosford Street was sitting alone by the fire in the house. A man dressed in black (as she says) came and sat down by her, and, after saying something to her, added that if she disclosed it she should thereupon die; and then left her.
>
> The next day the same person met her as she was coming down the stairs, and asked her, whether she had divulged what he before said, which she answered in the negative. He, after repeating the threat again, left her.
>
> The girl has had intermitting fits ever since, and will not disclose what was said to her. Whether this was a supernatural being (which some imagine), or a trick by some human person, or a phantom of her own, we shall not pretend to determine.

The hospital ghost, Stoney Stanton Road

The Coventry and Warwickshire Hospital on the Stoney Stanton Road dates back to the nineteenth century, though much of it belongs to the twentieth century. The hospital is thought to be haunted by a nurse who is seen occasionally around the wards. Tom Reale of Bell Green recalls an incident there a few years ago when he worked as an engineer at the hospital. He stated:

I was employed there as a maintenance engineer for many years and my job was to maintain all hospital equipment. I remember one week in January when it was my turn to be on call during the night and I got called out at 9.30 to a breakdown in one of the operating theatres. Now we only used theatres at night for emergencies so there was only a skeleton staff on duty during the night, namely one night sister and one theatre porter and one theatre porter/technician.

The machine I was called out to repair is called an 'autoclave' which is used to sterilise instruments and theatre packs. I checked the machine, found the fault and repaired it, then put the machine through a test run. I sat down with my back to the door. These doors are heavy wooden doors, two inches thick with an eighteen-inch window. They were kept closed by a closing device which operates automatically ensuring they are closed all the times during operations.

The Coventry and Warwickshire Hospital during the Blitz.

The only lights I had switched on were the corridor and sterilising room lights, so everywhere else was in darkness and all I could hear was the sound of the machine as it did the test run. Between its different cycle changes it was silent running. As I was sitting watching the machine I suddenly got a strange feeling that I was being watched. I got up and as I turned around I saw the heavy door behind me slowly closing.

I called out 'Who is there?' and got no answer so I went to the theatres and switched on the lights, nobody there, went through the scrub-up room into the anaesthetic rooms, nobody there. Crossed the corridor to the other theatre, no-one there. I went through every room and nobody was to be seen. It was so still and eerie you could hear a pin drop. I went back to the sister's office and asked her if she had been down to the theatre, she said no she had not. She asked why and I told her what happened and she said it could be Dave the night porter/technician who sometimes came in early and walked around checking things.

I thought no more of it, went back and finished the job, then went back to change from my sterile clothes when Dave arrived to change for work. So if Dave or the sister had not been there who had been watching me? It was a strange experience. I mentioned it to some of the nurses next day and one of them said she had heard that it was haunted by the ghost of a nurse who had worked there and who I knew well and she had died several years previously.

'Old Nick's Tree', the Mill Dam, Pool Meadow

The area now covered by Millennium Square was once part of a large lake which stretched towards Pool Meadow. The lake was fed by the Radford Brook and the Sherbourne and was originally part of a large lake which stretched between Broadgate and Barr's Hill. This shrank down centuries ago leaving what was once St Osburg's Pool and a later reduced version was known as the 'Mill Dam' as it ran the waterwheel of the mill of Coventry's Priory.

In the past the area around the pool was said to be haunted by people who had drowned there. One such was recorded in 1888 by T.W. Whitley who said that 100 years previously a man's wife had disappeared with their baby one night and 'they procured a lighted lantern, and with the help of some neighbours a search was made, and the water of the mill pool dragged, when, at last, something was seen floating on the surface of the pool, which on being got out was found to be the lifeless body of the unfortunate woman, but the baby was not found till the following morning, having floated on to the roots of a large ash tree on the other side of the pool, where it was taken out alive.'

The area the woman was found in was near a narrow causeway which ran alongside of the lake near to St Agnes Lane. This area is now covered by Hales Street and the Transport Museum. The area where the child was recovered was near what was until recently the site of the Smithfield Hotel, which itself had a reputation of being haunted by an actor who died there.

The ash tree in question was not an ordinary tree for it was said the devil himself once rested in it. A tale has it that some 'ill-disposed persons' tried to raise the devil in the nearby grammar school. After symbols were marked into the floor and magical incantations called, his satanic majesty appeared inside the building before the people. No sooner had he manifested, he leapt crashing through the window and came to rest at the side of the lake on the ancient ash tree. It is said that as the devil sat, his sheer weight made the branches groan as they sunk down towards the water. Thereafter it was said that on windy nights the old ash would moan horribly unlike any other tree and that was how it came to be called 'Old Nick's Tree'.

The edge of the Mill Dam, scene of many tragedies and Old Nick's Tree, an ancient ash tree on the right.

Interestingly most ancient trees which later became associated with the devil were sacred in pagan times. The ash itself was sacred to the Saxons and was associated with the god Woden. In Norway was one great sacred ash which stood by a lake and a sacred small pool in which human sacrifices were made. Again interestingly, a few hundreds yards from Old Nick's Ash was Hob's Hole. Hob is of course the name of a demon. Here at Hob's Hole a ritual was carried out until the nineteenth century in which a man was elected as Mayor of Hob's Hole. The ritual ended when the 'mayor' was carried shoulder high and thrown into the paved pool. This mirrored the pagan ritual of putting a sacrificial victim into the water so they would pass into the world of the gods. Such sites were in later Christian times often demonised and associated with the devil or demons.

The artisan and the spirits

Joseph Gutteridge was a noteworthy nineteenth-century Coventry artisan who was not only a skilled weaver but also a man of many parts with many interests, including natural history, geology and spiritualism. He wrote his autobiography telling the trials and successes of his life, called *Light and Shadows in an Artisan's Life*. One chapter was based on the growing nineteenth-century interest in spiritualism. Gutteridge had an open mind on the existence of spirits and believed that since so many eminent men believed in it, it was worthy of investigation.

Joseph Gutteridge, the artisan who attended séances and who claimed his bed was lifted three times by spirits.

Cook Street, also known as Tower Street, where Gutteridge lived and held his first séances.

Gutteridge attended popular table-tapping sessions and said of them that 'phenomena occurred in our presence, such as violent rockings and upheavals of a table, and many movements of heavy articles of furniture diametrically opposed to the law of gravity, with raps and concussions that seemed powerful enough to split the furniture into fragments.'

He continued to experiment with the phenomena in 1849 in his house in Tower Street (Cook Street). Of this he wrote, 'A "circle" around a table being recommended as the best method of encouraging spiritual phenomena... Nothing more than the tilting of the table and the tapping underneath occurred for a long time, but these could not be accounted for. The only point on which we were satisfied was that they were not produced voluntarily by any of those present. The table moved with our hands placed above it without actual contact.'

Gutteridge says that séances were held at the house of Mr Rodhouse, who lived at the corner of the Star Yard in Earl Street. He attended one of the meetings 'in a more than ordinarily sceptical mood, determined to ferret out fraud'. Gutteridge demanded some evidence to prove the genuineness of the medium and this he said was given through the medium – who was an illiterate boy – telling him things concerning his mother and father only known to himself.

Gutteridge also mentions an unusual event which happened when he moved to his new home in Yardley Street, which appeared to be haunted by a spirit either already there or invited through séances. He says, 'The bed on which we lay was lifted bodily up, so that with a pencil I might have written upon the ceiling, the motion being so gentle that it was scarcely perceivable; we were let down as gently, so that it was impossible to tell by any jarring sensation when the floor was reached. This was attempted a second time, though we were not taken so high. My wife says a third attempt was made, but I must have gone to sleep, for I did not notice it. On another occasion I saw two venerable-looking figures at the foot of the bed, and asked my wife if she saw them, but she did not... I was puzzled, being perfectly wide awake.'

At one séance in his house, Gutteridge says fresh flowers were brought by the spirits. He says, 'It was early spring, when the daffodils were beginning to appear. At the commencement of the sitting the weather outside was fine, but while we were indoors a snowstorm came on. None of the sitters came in or went out during the séance... At one point during the sitting I felt distinctly a soft velvety hand pushed into mine, which was closed. I grasped the hand; it melted away, and left behind two daffodils... Flowers and freshly gathered leaves of plants were also showered upon the table in the centre of the room, fifteen or sixteen different species, covered with melted snow...'

On another occasion he says, 'fruit was brought into the room by spirits. At a house in Bath Street, a medium named Fellows, prohibited by spirit friends from drinking during the séances, and persisting in the practice, set a jug of ale and glass on the table, and during the meeting, while another medium was in control, poured out a glass of the liquid. On raising it to his lips to drink, it was a solid mass, and would not leave the glass. It remained solid until the close of the meeting... This solidification of the ale was witnessed by myself and a number of others...'

Of these surprising events Gutteridge writes, 'It has been my lot to witness many occurrences which to persons unacquainted with spiritualism would be considered marvellous, but which, among those who have investigated the phenomena, are ordinary events.'

The skull, St John's Street

Coventry has suffered on a number of occasions in its history from visitations of the Black Death or plague. During one fourteenth-century visitation the prior's tenants in the north of Coventry

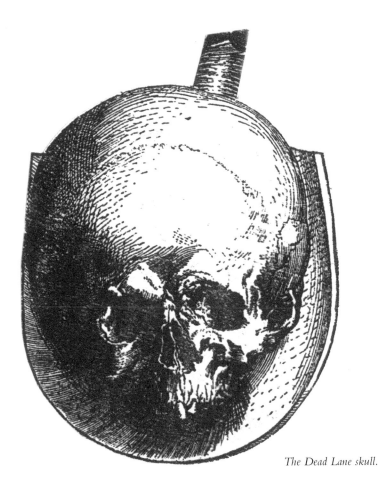

The Dead Lane skull.

were decimated by an outbreak which eventually took the prior himself. One version of the City Annals states that in 1349 'the living scarcely sufficed to bury the dead'. During another visitation in the seventeenth century many people left the city and built themselves temporary housing in the Great Park near to Quinton Pool.

Of those who died we are told that fields were acquired outside the city to bury the dead. Other stories tell of them being taken miles outside the city for burial. One local tradition however persists telling of a mass burial inside the city, beside the city wall, in a hollow adjoining the then footpath leading from New Gate to the Great Park. In nearby St John's Street it is said that during one visitation the plague wiped out the entire street, bar one family. Ever since this terrible event it was known as Dead Lane.

We are informed that in the late nineteenth century a landlord of a public house in St John's Street was digging his garden when he noticed that the ground below him gave a hollow ring. He dug down deeper and unearthed a large skull and a great number of bones. He took the skull into the pub and, much against his wife's consideration, he placed it upon the mantelpiece in the pub parlour.

That night, soon after going to bed their sleep was disturbed by strange noises coming from downstairs as if someone was moving about in the bar. The landlord ignored the sound, assuming that it was something to do with the cat, but his wife kept pushing him to go down and look. As the noises got louder he could no longer ignore her pleas and went to investigate. He searched, but nothing untoward could be found so he returned to his slumber.

No sooner had he settled than the noise restarted, this time louder than before, with a fast and furious rapping. He returned for a second time and this time came to the conclusion that the skull was to blame. So still in his nightshirt and by lamplight he returned to his backyard and re-buried the skull deep down where he had found it. He then returned to bed and a quiet night passed and, as long as the skull rested, the noises did not return.

The Cranes Inn apparition, Bishop Street

There are few really old ghost stories recorded in Coventry; this one, however, was recorded on 8 May 1810 and took place at the Cranes Inn, which stood on Bishop Street until 1940 when it was totally destroyed by a single high-explosive bomb.

The apparition, as it was called, was recorded on a handbill which was sold on the streets of Coventry. It was entitled 'A Supposed Apparition' and read:

On Monday night last, after some part of the soldiers belonging to the local militia, quartered at the Cranes Inn, had retired to bed. One of them was wonderfully surprised and alarmed by a somewhat unknown appearance, which glanced by the besides of him in particular. Who being awakened saw the dreadful appearance in a flame of fire! Bearing in one hand something unknown.

Cranes Inn (left), looking down Bishop Street. (Chris Barnes)

After a short space of time, it exclaimed, 'Mosely! Mosely! Mosely! Being the name of the person then in bed. The man not knowing what to say, he called out 'Brother! Brother!' but after some time considering, he thought it was the devil, from an apprehension of having said or done something serious.'

The ghost that wasn't

Coventry's Belgrade Theatre in Corporation Street was the first purpose-built theatre in post-war Britain. In any discussion of ghosts in Coventry the Belgrade will be mentioned. It is said that the theatre is haunted by the ghost of its first director, who died in a car crash. That said, ghost stories are like other stories, they are not always based on reality; this appears to be the case with the Belgrade for, according to the present director, the story of the theatre's ghost is a fabrication. He states that the story of the first director was made up as part of a ghost story competition and that it is now part of the theatre's folklore. That said, various individuals who have worked at the Belgrade in the past claim that there was indeed a ghost backstage!

The Prince Consort and the cycle

E.W. Cooper was the assistant of James Starley, the 'Father of the Cycle', and it was he who rode the first imported cycle in Coventry, which caused a sensation in the city streets. Cooper wrote his autobiography in 1928 which is mainly about his life as a cycle pioneer. Amongst his reminiscences are tales of a more spiritual nature, i.e. ghosts and spirits.

Cooper's first story dates back to before he was born:

It happened when my father was away from home for a week or so on a journey connected with canal traffic, and one night my mother was roused by a knocking, she said on the board near her head. She was thoroughly awakened by it, and heard then a loud rough voice cry, 'Gi'es yer hond! Gi'es yer hond!' Then there was silence, but turning her eyes towards the head of the bed, where she first heard the knocking, she saw a bright light on the headboard, that when she held her hand in it, it showed her fingers quite clearly.

My mother as I knew her was quite without fear. She jumped out of bed to investigate, and after satisfying herself that there was no moon or any light that could come from the window, got into bed as the light faded away, and went to sleep again. The knocking was repeated each night until my father came home, but she said she got quite used to it.

She was quite puzzled about the cry, 'Gi'es yer hond' … until my father related a narrow escape from drowning he had while away. One night, he said, while their boat was passing through a lock of the canal, he fell into the water and got drawn under the boat. In rising he felt, he said, the boat moving over his head and knew if he tried to reach the surface … his head might get crushed… He had to lie under the water … and he felt ready to burst … when, as he rose to the surface, someone learned over shouting, 'Gi'es yer hond!' and pulled him to safety. My mother smiled to herself and told him of the cry she had heard in the night, and which proved to be on the same date as his terrible experience.

E.W. Cooper in the early twentieth century.

The 'Father of the Cycle', James Starley.

After his father had returned Cooper says:

> The first night of my father's return my mother lay awake wondering if the rapping would come, when tap, tap, tap, tap came on the bed's head. 'What's that?' said my father. 'Go to sleep,' said mother. 'I am used to it.' The next night both lay awake waiting for the rapping and they came, but louder and at other parts of the room.
>
> My father could not stand it and jumped out of bed, struck a light, and began to search the room, the noises still continuing. My two brothers were awakened, and all joined in the search. Although noises were heard all around … nothing could be seen, or the din accounted for. This was repeated so often that they were compelled to leave the house, which they did at short notice… It all happened before I came on the scene, yet those concerned were ever ready to vouch for its accuracy.

During the period in the 1860s and '70s when Cooper acted as assistant to the great inventor and cycle manufacturer James Starley, he said his friend was lodging with some people, who were 'sperret rappers'. Cooper advised his friend to find new lodgings, as he believed it was generally all fake. Cooper's friend begged him to come and see the 'table perform'. Of this Cooper wrote:

> The whole thing seemed so ridiculous that I lost my patience and told him that if I did come I would expose the fraud… After persistent invitations I had at last promised to go, for his sake. He was a decent fellow, and I felt sorry that he was being deluded.
>
> At the table tipping session a labouring man asked his dead grandfather questions and the table tipped a number of times depending on the answer. The grandfather was asked what time was on Cooper's watch which his normally kept five minutes fast. The answer was correct but Cooper was unimpressed and left.

Sometime later another colleague talked Cooper into attending a séance held by his sister who he claimed had real powers. Cooper agreed, ready again if necessary to expose fraud. He wrote:

> Without ceremony of any sort I was introduced to his wonderful sister of 40hp mediumship, who, without preparation of any kind sat down, and placing her hands on the large square kitchen table, bade me to do the same, her brother following suit… Very soon rappings were heard, apparently on top of the table… The light was full on… I asked them or it if it could rap directly under my hands [which it did]… I further asked could they move the table? Thinking this was a poser as it had four legs and was also square topped and heavy. In a few minutes essayed a slow kind of hornpipe [dance], each of its legs taking part in turn.

This séance got Cooper more intrigued and he wished to 'investigate' other spirit rappers, who he says, 'had got quite a footing in the city'. Cooper talked the one medium into giving him a night a week in which he would be in full control. The first sitting he says was at her house, this he cut short. He does however say that a later séance proved more interesting.

Cooper had had cards printed and asked the table to tip when he pointed to the appropriate letter which would eventually spell a word. This was done so he could see to it that the medium could not influence the event. Cooper convinced Starley himself to accompany him to the séance for the sake of science and Starley came. Cooper wrote that:

Left: *The Prince Consort when he first married Victoria. Albert is believed to have contacted James Starley from the other side.*

Below: *Part of Far Gosford Street in the 1920s.*

Through the tipping and pointing to cards, a 'message' was given out to be read by 'Mr Starley' alone. I can picture his face now as, after reading it, looking at me, he said, 'This is private and incomprehensible too, as no-one but myself knows anything of this.'

To be brief it related to an invention he had been working out in secret at the time. I saw the 'message' myself, which said word for word as near as possible; 'Mr Starley, we are interested in your latest idea. It will be a success. I will use my influence in the highest quarters in the land. – P.C.' Jokingly, I suggested P.C. stood possibly for police constable, and asked could they give a full name. At once the answer came –'Prince Consort'.

Cooper was amazed and said he would sooner it meant 'Peter Common'. The interesting thing about this tale is that Starley was indeed working on a secret design for his Salvo Quad cycle. No sooner had the new cycle been completed than Starley received a message from Buckingham Palace. Queen Victoria, the grieving wife of Albert – the Prince Consort – wanted two of Starley's Salvo Quads.

Starley personally accompanied the machines to Buckingham Palace and Queen Victoria gave him an engraved silver watch and a royal warrant. What she said to Starley we do not know but we do know that Victoria spent many hours at the séance table in contact with her beloved Albert.

The ghost of Far Gosford Street

Many of Coventry's old streets and courts would have been full of tales of hauntings, but sadly few have survived; one which has is the ghost of Far Gosford Street. The *Midland Daily Tribune* reported on 26 June 1930 that, 'Strange tappings and a phantom figure are stated to have been seen in the middle of the night, and have terrified a family, occupying an old house – 36 Far Gosford Street.'

The house in question was probably quite crowded as it was occupied by a Mrs M. Rickhuss, her sons Sam and Jack and her daughters Sarah and Joan. It was also shared with her son-in-law Mr Turner, who was married to her eldest daughter, and they also had two children. A reporter noted that an unusual feature of the house was that a large number of its doors and cupboards had been bricked in.

This same reporter tells us that:

During the last few months Mr Turner states he heard tapping noises from the cupboard on the stairs near the first floor bedroom where the boys sleep. Not long ago they were all awoken by screams in the middle of the night, and Sam was found to be sat up in bed in hysterics. He said he had seen a ghost, 'An old gentleman with a long white beard and outstretched arms. He peered at me from the bottom of the bed.'

Sam thereafter refused to sleep in the room and was so affected that he had to receive medical attention. His father also confirmed that he too had seen the old man in his bedroom and it appeared after the tapping sounds got clearer. It was reported that the house was thoroughly searched, including the lifting of the floorboards, but no explanation could be found. The Far Gosford Street ghost then disappeared into the mists of time.

The flower shop – ghost or timeslip?

The *Coventry Evening Telegraph* of 22 December 1978 informs us of an incident which took place in an upstairs room of the 'Floral Charm Shop', a flower shop in the Burges. The shop was due to close and Pauline Kiedron of Keresley told a reporter that as she was about to go upstairs to the stockroom, she had her hand on the door handle and suddenly had a strange experience of feeling that she was already in the stockroom.

She recalled what she saw:

In the middle of the room was a high-backed chair without arms. Sitting in it was a little boy of about six or seven years dressed in a black velvet pageboy suit, with knee breeches and buckled shoes. He had shoulder-length wavy, mousey-coloured hair, but I could not see his face – it was like a light bulb that is not switched on. His hands were loosely folded in his lap and his feet did not reach the floor. I saw it all clearly in a spilt second and yet I had not moved from the ground floor. The stockroom is in regular use and of course, there is no such chair in it.

The parson's ghost, Grove Street

Just off Cox Street in Grove Street, which has since been demolished, was the printing shop of Parbury Brothers. The building had not always been a printing works, for it began life in Victorian times as a Primitive Methodist Chapel. The building appears to have been taken over by Parbury's around 1898. Things, however, quickly came to the notice of the men who worked the machines and strange tales began to emerge.

In the early 1960s these tales began to reach the press and the *Coventry Standard* sent forth a 'lady reporter' to investigate. She first spoke to Steve Cooke, the foreman, who told her that he had experienced a number of strange events over the last twelve months. We are told that Steve 'took our reporter upstairs to the little gallery that runs round three walls of the chapel. "Several times when I have been working in the corner of the gallery I have heard footsteps up the stairs," he said. "They have reached the landing at the top, shuffled their feet – but when I have turned around there is nothing there."'

It was said that bones were found underneath the building when it was being set up as a print shop and Mr Cooke suggested that it may have been built on a graveyard. Miss Beattie Bates, who at that time had worked in the former chapel for thirty-five years, told the reporter that she hadn't experienced anything, but she knew many who had. Her strangest tale concerning the building involved the disappearance of two large Coronation pictures which apparently vanished overnight from the locked building and were never seen again. However, this was surely as a result of human, rather than ghostly, intervention!

She did however tell of an ex-employee saying, 'that he often felt a hand on his shoulder as he was working at a particular machine.' Several others said they often felt someone brushing by them as they worked. All assumed in the end that the spirit who wandered the building was of an old parson who preached here. Those who worked the machine by where the pulpit once stood were apparently 'touched' the most.

Miss Bates recalled, 'The worst time is after five o'clock.' She recalled one employee who was almost scared out of his wits one dark night while working overtime. 'He told me that he

Parbury's printing works in Cox Street was housed in a building much like this other old Coventry Baptist chapel.

distinctly felt someone – or something – standing right behind him. But of course, when he looked round there was nothing there.'

Although there were no definite sightings of a ghostly parson, the paper states that 'when several independent normal men and women talk in a tone which is quietly convincing ... one cannot help wondering whether there are presences which are more than imagination.'

The Starley ghost

The ghost in question here is actually the nephew of James Starley, who received the message from Prince Albert. Vera Padbury was in a pottery class in a building on the corner of Vine Street, Hillfields in what was then an annex to the Coventry Polytechnic and later a community centre. All was normal until she suddenly became aware of a man standing close by. She thought the man unusual and grim; he stood there with his hands behind his back looking into the room. She turned to draw her friends' attention to him, but when she looked back the stranger was gone.

Vera said that the man wore a grey tweed suit, with waistcoat and watch chain and had a thick moustache and sideburns. His appearance didn't initially register as Vera was more drawn to the expression on his face. She said, 'He had a frown on his face, as if he was wondering what we were all doing there.' Nobody but Vera saw the man and someone suggested that perhaps a clue as to who he was may be on one of the four plaques outside the building.

Above left: *John Kemp Starley, who was thought to have been seen in the Vine Street building.*

Above right: *The building on the corner of Vine Street.*

She recognised one name – John Kemp Starley, nephew of James Starley. He had been the president of the Coventry and District Sunday School Union, who used the building in the 1890s. Vera was afterwards shown a picture of J.K. Starley and was convinced that it was the man she had seen for a fleeting moment during her pottery class.

John Kemp Starley worked, like his uncle, in the cycle trade and invented the 'Rover' safety cycle, the forerunner of modern cycles. His firm later became Rover Cars. Starley lived at Barrs Hill House, Radford Road, and died there aged forty-seven in 1902. His house was later converted into Barrs Hill School, which sadly was afterwards knocked down and turned into a car park.

It seems hard to say why Starley would haunt the Vine Street building. The fact that he appeared as a solid figure may suggest that what Vera saw was a flash from the past, a time slip, meaning Starley wasn't a ghost but alive and in his own time. No-one can explain how time works, but sometimes people see fleeting glimpses of things that belonged to other times, usually the past. Perhaps the most famous case of this was when a retired police officer saw a Roman army marching through the crypt of York Minster along what was in their time a Roman road. They passed through the crypt totally oblivious to what was around, indicating that they were in their own time. Perhaps John Kemp Starley had stood in the schoolroom in the late 1890s and was for a split-second puzzled by a vision of strangely dressed people making pottery. Who knows!

TWO

SPECTRES IN THE SUBURBS

The Earlsdon ghost

Providence Street in Earlsdon contains many fine houses, but one building now used as an office once had a bit of a reputation. Mrs Merchant recalled her memories of the building first in the *Echo*. Thanks to her and the *Echo* I repeat her story here:

When I was a child I lived in Earlsdon in a house which I remember with little affection and which has haunted my dreams… The house in question was one my parents took my sister and me to live in when they returned to Coventry after the Second World War … the garden was lovely. There were apple trees, a mass of climbing roses, both white and red … the garden was a joy; but how I grew to hate the chill, sunless house, and the nights spent there.

I had nightmares many nights. At least I was told they were bad dreams. 'Just a dream' my father would say, when he came to me in response to my nocturnal calls, and with irritation increasing with the frequency of these events. Even the doctor was consulted. 'The child is over-imaginative,' he pronounced, 'nothing to worry about'. My parents were relieved by his authoritative dismissal; I was isolated.

I pleaded to be allowed to sleep with the light on. A bedside lamp was purchased. Although I was able to fall asleep happily, my parents would turn it off once I was asleep. When darkness fell and the bedroom was in shadows, she, and I knew it was an old woman, would appear; dark, still and staring. Staring without face or eyes. A pitch black shape that generated a relentless staring sensation. Sometimes she was at the foot of my bed, or by the door, or silhouetted against the window. I would cry out till my father came. 'Another bad dream', he would say again. Except I knew I had not been asleep.

The worst time was when I woke up and saw the shape reclining on the spare bed in my room as if supported on one elbow. This time I just met its stare. I was rigidly transfixed, trapped, unable to call out or reach for the light switch. I don't remember how I eventually broke the spell, but I long remembered the fear I felt.

Time passed and I learned to deal with my 'dreams' by reciting a protective prayer I'd learned at Sunday school… Eventually we moved to another house where I slept soundly and happily and, incidentally, in the darkness… Years later, I decided to ask my mother about the nature of the illness she suffered while we lived at that house. I believed it to be some sort of nervous breakdown.

'What do you think caused you to go to pieces, Mum,' I asked. 'It seems so silly now,' she replied dismissively, 'but I thought the house in Providence Street was haunted.' I went back to look at the house with my sister... I became uncomfortable at its sight... 'I don't like this place at all, I wish I hadn't come back,' my sister said. 'Mum thought it was haunted,' my words came unbidden. 'So do I.'

We compared experiences, they were so similar. We were both aware that the presence we had encountered was a woman and always in the same room in the house. We recalled how our dog had sometimes inexplicably growled when she lay at the foot of the stairs, as if disturbed by something at the head of them.

We were always a practical down-to-earth family, so I ran these ideas past my father, fully expecting him to dismiss the whole notion. He didn't scoff at all but gave some detail of my mother's experience of an old woman whom she had encountered in the same room in which I had slept. He also recalled investigating the sighting of 'someone upstairs' by my sister and he too recalled our dog's behaviour, so out of character to his normal placid, friendly, stranger-licking behaviour.

Wanting to know the background to the house, Mrs Merchant spent some time researching in the City Record Office and discovered in the 1891 census that the house belonged to a watch dial painter called Charles. Charles appears to have died shortly after the First World War leaving his wife Fanny with three children. The children grew up and left Fanny alone in the house, in which she died.

Mrs Merchant says that, 'The watchmaker cottage is now used as offices. I wonder if, when the lights are turned off and everyone has gone to their bright, welcoming homes, a lone dark shape silently reclaims that upstairs room, and sightlessly stares at the usurpation of her home by others.'

Ghosts of Binley churchyard and tunnel

The present eighteenth-century Adams-style church was built by Lord Craven of nearby Coombe Abbey. It was not the original church on this site for an older building, originally a twelfth-century chapel, previously stood here. I am not aware that the church is haunted but it has been claimed that the churchyard is. Strange as it may seem, despite what they contain, few churchyards can claim to be haunted by the dead, more likely by the living pretending to be the dead.

A cutting from the *Coventry Standard* states:

On the night of 29 January 1961 two Coventry youths were taking a short cut through the same churchyard at Binley, sometime around 9.00 p.m. when in front of them materialised a figure in a long cloak with a luminous head. The youths – badly frightened – ran away from it as fast as they could. The next night, having overcome their fright, they visited the churchyard again at the same time, taking with them a camera to photograph the apparition should it materialise again. Sure enough it did. It had the same appearance about it as on the Sunday night – a long cloak with spikes protruding from its neck.

The interior of the Adams-style Binley Church built on the site of a medieval church.

A photograph of it was taken but on the film being developed (not by them) it was found to be blank. In passing, it may be noted that the youths had no idea of any ghosts at Binley; not until afterwards was it widely known that some ghostly manifestation had, it seemed taken place some forty years before they were born.

Sadly this event isn't recorded but it would have been useful to add something to this case.

Mr S. King, a former resident of Binley, wrote to me regarding the above event in February 2004 saying, 'It is certainly true though that several people believed that they at different times saw a ghostly figure in Binley churchyard about 1959; indeed the story was reported in the *Coventry Standard* at the time and many people subsequently turned up to 'see the phantom'. The ghost chose not to come out to play the night the crowd came, but a trio of young lads covered themselves in a sheet, entered the burialground at the far, unlit end, and proceeded to instil excitement, until one of the lads tripped over a gravestone and the prank was discovered.'

Mr King also remembered other stories including the tale of the tunnel from Coombe Abbey to Binley Vicarage, which tradition states was originally a farmhouse belonging to the monks. Most tunnel stories have little foundation but the daughter of an ex-worker on Coombe Estate told me her late father swore it was true and actually claimed to have been into the tunnel himself. According to Mr King a local tale claimed that on the day Coombe Abbey was taken by the Crown, up to forty monks escaped into the tunnel, which unbeknown to them had been sealed at the farmhouse/vicarage end. Then it is claimed the soldiers took the abbey and sealed the other entrance, trapping the monks inside. Subsequently as Mr King says, 'Some thirty or forty souls died over the subsequent days and weeks under horrendous conditions and their ghosts have been seen over the centuries by occupants of the vicarage. In the late 1950s some people still remember on visiting the vicarage seeing a human skull placed on a table at the entrance to the kitchen.'

Although there may be something in the tunnel story, the idea of the monks escaping through the tunnel doesn't ring true, for the monks of Coombe knew months in advance that their house was to be dissolved and had been promised pensions. However, practically none received them, assuming of course they were still alive!

Mr King also remembered other hauntings in Binley, one being around the old mill, down in Mill Lane:

A family named Brain lived next to the mill and at the mill six decades ago. They have long departed, but an ancestor of theirs was murdered by being sawn to death one bitter January night, and the pieces of his body were thrown into the Sowe. His screams and shrieks were said to mingle with the winter wind over the years.

The other haunted place was the land abandoned by the army which lay on the edge of Binley Little Wood, an area between Binley Pit Village and Brandon Road, now built over. It is said that a group of boys and girls could be seen holding hands, emerging from the wood and going together into the army blockhouses. But on subsequent investigation they could not be found. This is a story that was repeated in the 1960s by different individuals in Binley.

The gibbet, Gibbet Hill

Gibbet Hill was formerly known as Gallows Hill, for in some unknown period a person or persons were executed here. It got its present name from the fact that three men were hanged and gibbeted here for the murder of Stoneleigh farmer Thomas Edwards in 1765. The three men, dragoons Robert Leslie and Edward Drury and weaver Moses Baker, were hanged before a huge crowd then their bodies were taken down tarred and wrapped in chains and rehanged on the gallows. Here their remains were a landmark for forty-five years before what was left of them was removed. The gibbet itself with its rusty chain stood until it too was removed later in the nineteenth century. Parts of it were sold as souvenirs and the main frame was converted into the base of a hayrick at a nearby farm.

Not surprisingly Gibbet Hill gained a reputation of being haunted, although no specific stories really survive. It was said however that after the gibbet was removed, on windy nights you could still hear the old gibbet creak under its ghastly load.

One story survives that shortly after the execution a group of men drinking in a Coventry inn were discussing the event and a bet was laid that no-one would dare to go up to the gibbeted men at midnight and ask them loudly how they were getting on. One man took on the bet and, filled with tales to get him spooked, he arrived in the wind and rain on Gibbet Hill and called out to the blackened, chained bodies, 'How are you getting on up there?' Much to his surprise and horror a reply came: 'Very wet and cold.' This was enough to send him scurrying back to Coventry in terror filled with the belief that the dead criminals had spoken to him. However it was later pointed out that this was not really the case, as the spectral voice came from one of his drinking pals who had got there before him and secreted himself in a bush near to the gibbet. A similar story exists referring to the execution of Mary Ann Higgins on Whitley Common.

About fifteen years ago a friend of mine was driving up towards Gibbet Hill when he suddenly saw in front of him a group of young men fighting. In the blink of an eye they disappeared and he swore that it was not possible if these were real people. Where he saw this multiple apparition was near the bottom of Gibbet Hill in the area where William Law was fatally stabbed in 1818

Left: *Gibbet Hill. The site of the triple gibbet was a few yards down on the right. William Law met his fate at the bottom of the hill in the distance.*

Below: *A double gibbet. Gibbet Hill had a triple gibbet!*

after he and his friends were jumped by a group of Coventry youths with sticks. William was carried to the Windmill Inn which stood near to the present Leamington Road junction and there in agony he died.

The haunted farmhouse, Blackberry Lane

Green Farm in Blackberry Lane, Stoke Heath is a listed building, part of which dates back to 1675. In 1987 the building (which had stood empty for twenty-six years) was run down and threatened with demolition until self-employed builder John MacDonald saw its potential and acquired it himself. With grants and thousands of pounds of their own money, John and his wife Ann lovingly restored the old building and made it a family home again.

The approach to Jeffrey Woods Cross as it appeared in the beginning of the twentieth century. (Coventry City Libraries)

There is however something unusual about the building as *Coventry Evening Telegraph* reporter Andy Gilbert found out when he interviewed the family back in 1991. He pointed out that despite the many rooms, John and Ann's daughters, Mirelle and Marie, refused to sleep in one particular room because of two incidents.

Mirelle, aged thirteen at the time, said, 'I was in bed one night with just a bit of light coming through the window. I saw a man, woman and little child wearing old-fashioned clothes all pointing at me.' Her nine-year-old sister Marie had a similar experience some time later.

Their mother Ann hadn't seen anything herself but said, 'The house alarm keeps going off for no apparent reason. We kept a record and found it went off at 11.20 p.m. on 26 May both this year and last. Perhaps the strangest time though was when we first looked round this place.' While they were inside, the front door slammed shut trapping the couple inside and Ann recalled, 'We couldn't get out and John had to call to neighbours to rescue us.'

The haunted crossroads, Swan Lane

The junction of Harnall Lane East, Swan Lane, Burlington Road and Nicholls Street used to be known as Jeffrey Woods Cross. This once a rural road junction which was the meeting place of Harnall Lane and Swan Lane (originally called Tew's Lane) and had a reputation of being haunted by a suicide who was buried here. The person in question is said to be Jeffrey or Geoffrey Wood. This may be a young man who poisoned himself in West Orchard in March 1810. The young man in question had enlisted in the army, then changed his mind and couldn't procure a discharge; in desperation he took his own life. A jury brought a verdict of suicide and his body was conveyed through huge crowds on the back of a cart and was buried without ceremony in the roadway in Harnall Lane.

This suicide was buried with all the rites associated with that form of death, this being that the body would be buried in a roadside grave, or in the centre of the road, pinned into its last resting place with stakes or iron pins. This was done because it was believed that a suicide would rise from the grave and haunt; thus the pinning and the road junctions which were believed to confuse the spirit of the deceased and hold it in place. It is also possible that more than one suicide was buried at the junction. It is often noted that horses sometimes reacted when passing such places.

In any case, the area was believed to be haunted and the *Coventry Standard* of 6 April 1900 reported:

Not many years ago … there lived not far from … the crossroads … a superstitious family. They kept their doors locked at all hours of the day and night, lest perchance some goblin damned should find a way into the house; and when they did venture abroad, even in the daylight, they talked in whispers, with sidelong glances over their shoulders.

One member of the family owned a gun and had some sporting instincts, and he sometimes plucked up enough courage to go a mile or so away from home to shoot woodpigeons. It chanced one special occasion that he was belated; he did not reach home till a few minutes after midnight, and he was almost too breathless to speak and almost too nerveless to hold his gun.

When he had recovered his breath he told a wonderful story – how he was turning out of a lane towards the Cross, how he saw a horse and cart and a man in the cart coming along towards him. How the horse walked without making the least noise, how no rumble came from the cart, how when the middle of the crossroads was reached, the ground opened and the horse cart and man disappeared.

It is said that after this event members of this family getting braver would together go to Jeffrey Woods Cross at midnight to try to get a sighting of the apparition. They declared to others that they didn't just see it once but on numerous occasions, but it is said nobody believed them. Despite this all the family maintained that it was the truth.

'Spectator' wrote in the *Coventry Standard* on 9 March 1906 with more detail on the event as seen by others:

It used to be said [forty years earlier] that on certain nights of the year the burial of Geoffrey Wood took place on the exact lines of the tradition, with extras. At midnight a cart would be seen to approach the spot with two or three men in it.

When the crossroads was reached the men alighted, dug a shallow grave, placed a body in it, drove a stake through the body, and then filled up the grave. Then instead of driving away, the cart and horse and men vanished. By some it was said that they sank into the earth, by others that they rose in the air and floated away.

The phantom hound, Whitmore Park, Keresley and Radford

For centuries now all around England people have seen spectral black dogs, huge black shaggy animals about the size of a pony with red or green glowing eyes. Even now those with the

A legendary black dog

The pumping station in Watery Lane; in the field beyond the legendary black dog was last seen.

knowledge advise people who see these supernatural creatures not to strike them, for like a ball of energy they explode in a flash. Bungay Church in Suffolk had a famous visitation of a black dog in the seventeenth century. It is said that the creature appeared during a service and ran through the church; one person who caught a glancing blow from the animal shrivelled up. As the huge black hound pushed the church door it claws burnt into the wood and the marks are still pointed out to this day.

There are only a couple of black dog legends in Warwickshire and one is based in the north of Coventry. The beast is said to roam in Keresley, up to Hounds Hill, the ancient Whitmore Park, the medieval hunting park of the Bishop of Coventry and part of Radford, taking in the ancient 'Dog Land' and Upper and Lower Shuckmoor – the demon's moor. The latter may also give the ancient name for Coventry's black dog, for 'Shuck' is the name used to describe such a beast in the east of England.

It was said that no-one would cross Whitmore Park at night for 'fear of the beast that walks there'. Although references in place names relating to the beast go back to the fourteenth century the first known recorded sighting is said to have been in the eighteenth century when a horseman was returning from a Keresley inn. The rider is said to have come face to face with the black dog and struck it with his riding crop. This resulted in the creature exploding in a flash, blowing the horseman off his horse and into a ditch. The man had the clothes burnt off his back and the horse was finally found two days later in a terrible state of shock.

Another story comes from the mid-nineteenth century, when a farmhand was taking two carthorses from the 'Long Close' in Bennett's Road North early one morning. As they were passing through the gate the horses suddenly froze to the spot and the farmhand struggled in vain to move them. Suddenly he became aware of the reason why, as in the stillness of the morning a huge shaggy black dog came padding down the lane. All were frozen to the spot as the creature slowly passed by, turning its head towards the farmhand and showing it huge teeth in a ghastly grin. The creature passed by and then walked through the hedgerow, disappearing in a flash of exploding white light as it did so. Sometimes such sightings were said to portent the death of someone and in this case it is said that later in the morning the farmhand found his master had died.

The last time this legendary creature was seen, that I am aware of, was in 1949 by a Mr Jackson who worked at the pumping station in Watery Lane, Keresley. Mr Jackson told me that one night at 2.00 a.m. as he was crossing the Top Meadow after checking the pump he was stopped in his tracks by a huge black dog, which sat staring at him. After pulling himself together from the shock he slowly edged around it shining the light of his box lamp in its eyes. When I asked the then eighty-year-old gentleman how big the creature was, he said, 'It was sat on its haunches and it was bigger than me and I'm five foot ten.' Once past the creature he ran as fast as he could back to the station and locked himself in until the following morning, unlocking the door only when his mate came to relieve him. He told his workmate about the creature and was told that he too had thought he had seen something in the field. Later that morning a gent who lived next door called out to them, 'What sort of creature you had round here then?' They went around the back of his house and outside the kitchen window in the soft earth was a pad print Mr Jackson claimed was 'about the size of a dinner plate'. I was told this in the 1980s. Mr Jackson had never told anyone else but his wife about his sighting of the black dog for, as he said at the time, 'What would be the point, no-one would believe me!'

The creature was generally forgotten about but was remembered again in the 1930s when Keresley worthy Alfred Harris brought the story back to life, although now linking the black dog with the story of the ghost of Edward Broome saying, that it was Broome's dog.

The ghost of Edward Broome

In a part of Keresley called Penny Park stands a fine stone farmhouse now split into two. The building was once known as Penny Park House and is linked to the story of a gentleman farmer called Edward Broome, who (so the story goes) was hanged in a nearby barn in the sixteenth century. The story goes that the then owner of the farm at that time was one John Shore and he had invited a number of local worthies to his home to witness his engagement to Elizabeth Sadler of Newland Hall. Another of his guests was Edward Broome, who also had his eye on Elizabeth.

As Elizabeth Sadler rode to the house with her servants it is said she was accosted by Broome, who begged her to elope with him. There were raised voices when Elizabeth refused and Broome grabbed her horse's bridle. The surprised beast reared up, throwing her violently to the floor. As she lay seemingly dead Broome fled in a state of panic, followed by his faithful dog.

The beautiful Penny Park House as it is today.

RONALD FRANKEAU. One of the many who have been to Keresley to give a helping hand. The two photographs were taken at Keresley within a few minutes of each other. In the second he was " frightened by the ghost."

Ronald Frankeau

Seeing the Ghost

A photograph of Ronald Frankeau taken in 1942 before and after being 'frightened by the ghost' at Keresley.

Elizabeth was taken to Penny Park House believed by all to be dead and Shore gathered a group of men and went in pursuit of Broome. They quickly found him, for Broome was not trying to escape; his dog however would not let them take his master easily and died protecting him. Broome was finally taken back in silence to the barn at Penny Park and there Shore and the other men decided to take justice into their own hands and hanged Edward Broome from a chain.

Broome took some minutes to die as the chain slowly strangled him. The men shortly afterwards returned to the farm only to find that Elizabeth was not dead at all and they had just hanged an innocent man. A story was concocted that Broome in a state of 'drunkardness' had wandered into the barn and accidentally got entangled in the chain, an accident which ended his life. How the true story got out we do not know, but from then on Edward Broome's ghost was said to haunt the Keresley area.

The phantom coach, Tamworth Road

The Tamworth Road that heads north from Coventry is an old road, possibly even prehistoric as it passes by the ancient earthworks at Corley Rocks. Originally the Tamworth Road would have been little more than a dirt track but by the eighteenth century it was turnpiked from the Radford toll gate at the junction of Radford and Keresley Road to the second toll gate which stood where the Toll House pub stands at the split in the roads at Nether Whiteacre. The Turnpike Trust would have laid a half-decent road and maintained it using the fees paid by the passing traffic.

The road in the days of the Trust was very different to today, with people on foot and horseback passing by, sheep and cattle roaming and carts, carriages and coaches carrying passengers to Tamworth and beyond. Three pubs could be found as you left Coventry, the Shepherd and Shepherdess, the Fox Chase, which stood near the present Royal Court, and the Horse and Jockey at Corley.

It is near two of these old inns that something unusual has been seen, as David Stringer told me:

About ten years ago my son Paul was working as a local DJ and entertainer and on Bonfire Night he had a disco and firework display to do at Fillongley. He wanted to come straight home afterwards so he travelled there on his motorcycle. After he finished, at about midnight, he commenced his journey home along the Tamworth Road, towards Coventry, a road he knew reasonably well.

As he approached the Horse and Jockey, he saw, coming towards him, a dark stagecoach resplendent in all its livery, with driver, guard and four black horses. He thought it a little strange at that time of night but knowing the area he thought it was someone who had been to a horse show-type event and was just coming home late.

Right outside the Horse and Jockey the coach seemed to veer across the road towards him and he pulled over to avoid a collision. It came so close to him that he said he could have touched it. There appeared to be nothing wrong and he described it as being solid, not transparent and in full detail. After it had passed he continued on his journey but pondered on what he had seen. Something began to worry him as being not quite right and it soon dawned on him that, although passing very closely, there had been no noise, no horse's hooves, no rattle of wheels or anything, complete silence.

The Tamworth Road by the Horse and Jockey showing the original line of the road in front of the inn. The phantom coach swerved off the present main road, now running to the right.

When he arrived home he did not say anything to us, but the following morning something was obviously troubling him and after a lot of persuasion he told us the story. He was adamant as to what he had seen and could describe the coach and four horses in great detail.

Some months later I was talking to a colleague of mine and we started off discussing UFO sightings, but soon got round to strange incidents in general. I commenced to tell my friend about what my son had seen and he suddenly interrupted me saying, 'Don't tell me. He saw a black coach and four black horses!' 'Yes, how did you know?' I replied. 'My cousin saw the same thing a few years previous outside the Shepherd and Shepherdess pub, again on bonfire night.'

We were gobsmacked. We decided to do a bit of research to see if there was anything in history that might explain the sightings but nothing was found. Then a couple of years later I was at the Rainbow pub in Allesley with some family having a quiet drink on a lovely summer evening. The conversation got round to the history of the Rainbow and again I started to relate the bonfire night incidents, with, 'so there's two people that have seen the same thing'. My brother-in-law said, 'Three!' Obviously my question was, 'What do you mean?' He told me that a workmate of his tells the same story!'

David's son Paul recalls of the event, 'The coach was of the type seen in the films about highwaymen. I can't remember what the people looked like, but the horses were black with the one nearest to me having a white blaze on its forehead. The horses were also blinkered.' One interesting fact Paul recalls is that the coach didn't follow the present line of the road, but seemed to come across it, towards him. This made him believe that the road originally took a slightly different line, taking in the service road in front of the Horse and Jockey. This seems to make some sense as the present sweep of the road is more modern and the original course did run across the front of the pub. So the coach appears to have been following its original route.

Paul recalled that soon after his sighting the local BBC radio ran a feature on ghost stories and he rang in with his. He recalls several others also rang in saying they too had seen the phantom coach. I would like to imagine this phantom coach is the *Eclipse*, driven by Ned Hassall and guarded by Tom Peck. Hassall and Peck were two particularly well-known coaching men; Hassall was from Birmingham and Peck from Coventry. These two local characters spent years on the stagecoaches and were great friends. Their end came suddenly when one day they pulled in at the Craven Arms in the High Street. It had been frosty and Peck was lifting some luggage when he slipped backwards and cracked his head open on the pavement. He died on the spot. His great friend Hassall immediately fainted and was carried into the hotel. Hassall never got over the shock and died a raving lunatic in an asylum. It would be nice to imagine Peck and Hassall back together on their beloved coach going full gallop up the Tamworth Road, as they did in the good old days!

The 'ghost' on Whitley Common, London Road

At the turn of the nineteenth century there was scare over a strange apparition which was seen by a number of people on Whitley Common. In the darkness of night this apparition took the shape of strange nebulous blobs of white which glided in the air across the common and at the same time groaned and made coughing sounds. Then one day in the full light of day the mystery revealed itself as a coughing, asthmatic piebald cow. Having myself seen a black and white cow semi-lit by car headlights in a dark country lane near Napton some years ago, I know just how scary such a sighting as this can initially be! The common must have had a reputation for ghosts for again in the nineteenth century it is said that a driver of a carriage was terrified one misty night by a ghost with outstretched arms. This turned out to be a white finger-post.

Whitley Common itself has been the site of public executions in Coventry since at least the eighteenth century, so it is not surprising that it was thought to be haunted. One criminal, Thomas Wilday, a wool-comber, murdered his aunt Susannah Wall and her daughter at the White Lion in Smithford Street in 1734. Wilday, thinking his aunt had come into some money, knocked on the door of the inn of which she was the landlady and when she opened the door he rushed in and cut her throat. He went upstairs and came across her daughter Ann and to keep her silent he severed her head. He searched and found nearly £100 in gold and silver and left. This common murderer was quickly apprehended and soon confessed his foul deed. He was soon after hanged and gibbeted on Whitley Common. It is said that eventually the remains of his body were taken down and buried below the gibbet. Later it was said that his remains were dug up by workmen looking for sand and his bones were ground up with this sand to use in the mortar in the construction of Ryton Bridge. His ghost was said to have haunted the old bridge. If it haunts the present one I cannot say.

The old gallows mound near Howes Lane; one would excpect this to be the most haunted part of the common. This is part of the area where Mary Ann Higgins' ghost was said to have been seen.

A ghost that was said to actually haunt the common itself was that of Mary Ann Higgins, who was hanged on the common in 1831 for poisoning her uncle. It is that said certain individuals, who were poachers and who had actually witnessed Mary Ann being hanged, claimed that they would often see her ghost wandering the common wearing the same clothes she was hanged in. She was also seen down a nearby lane where in life she had walked with her sweetheart George Clarke, who by all accounts appears to have been involved in the murder.

It is said that on one occasion a drinker at the Crown Inn bet his fellow drinkers one gallon of ale that one of them would not go to the common at midnight to ask the ghost of Mary Ann Higgins how she was. What followed formed a standing joke for years. The man who took on the wager headed for the common along the London Road unaware that some of his fellow drinkers were already secreted there at the gallows site.

The man arrived and put forward the selected question, 'Mary Ann Higgins, how are you?' to which the answer came, 'Wet and Cold.' This reply had the desired effect and the man, frightened out of his wits, took to his heels and ran almost all the way back to the Crown, white as a sheet, shouting, 'I've seen her, I've seen her! I have seen Mary Ann Higgins' ghost and she told me she was wet and cold.'

This said, the company broke down in peals of laughter and the terrified man was brought back to earth hearing their confession. After the others retuned from the common the laughter broke out again, and eventually all were satisfied when the forfeit was upped to two gallons of ale which were quickly consumed on the premises.

Poltergeist in Delius Street, Tile Hill

The *Coventry Evening Telegraph* of 16 August 1988 reported scary goings-on in a house in Delius Street, Tile Hill. Debbie Flangham was so frightened by what was going on in her house that her friend Karen Peters moved in. It was reported that shoes moved on their own and things not only went bump in the night but also vanished and reappeared in other rooms. Weird choking noises were also heard in the middle of the night.

It was reported that the fire service was called after the electricity meter clocked up £60 in half an hour, this was despite the fact that the power was switched off at the time. Firemen waited while an electrician disconnected the meter. Karen said:

> It's weird, I don't know whether it's a poltergeist but it's definitely frightening. It's scaring the kids. The youngest has started talking to someone called Sarah – we don't know anyone called Sarah.
>
> Someone who was here saw a pair of shoes turn over on their own accord. And we heard all sorts of noises in the night. A bottle of anti-perspirant disappeared off the bathroom shelf and two days later turned up in the lounge. It was too high for any of the kids to reach it.

Her friend Debbie said, 'I've only been here two weeks and I like the place. But it's quite frightening. I don't know what to make of it.'

So disturbing were the events that the Revd Brian Doolan was called out and said prayers and sprinkled holy water. He told the reporter, 'I've been to two houses in the area over the last few days. In some circumstances the phenomena probably results from the soul of a departed person that cannot find rest. It may attach itself to a place which at some time in its life may have been important. It is a great and strange mystery.'

The Revd Doolan added that he was to get in touch with the bishop's advisor to see if further action was needed, such as exorcism. As for the fire service, fire sub-officer Peter Wallsgrove said, 'Apparently there was some sort of fault on the electric junction box. Don't expect me to explain the rest of it.' he said, 'we've never been called out to a poltergeist before.'

The haunted school, Coundon

In January 1909 industrialist, cycle pioneer, strong family man and ex-mayor George Singer died unexpectedly of a brain haemorrhage in bed at his home in Coundon Court, which is now Coundon Court School and Community College. Singer's sudden and unexpected demise left a legacy, for he seems to be unaware of his own death.

Ex-head of English Richard Hoare has been amongst the select few who have seen him. He recalls, 'In fact two of us saw him at the same time in a classroom on the top floor of the old house. It used to be his children's bedroom. He was standing by the far window looking out on the grounds. He turned towards us and just vanished! On a clear day he could have seen the three spires of Coventry. We like to think he returns to his children's bedroom for this reason and it was of course his favourite room.'

Richard said, 'He was in his late forties and he had a full beard. I knew the face well from old photographs. It was George Singer, around the time he was Mayor of Coventry in the 1890s.'

Above: *Coundon Court, home of George Singer and for many years a school.*

Left: *George Singer, industrialist and former Coventry mayor, is still seen in his former home.*

Two caretakers have also seen Singer, as has English teacher Janet Powell, who was alone in the house tidying up after a parents evening in 1992. She recalled that as she turned off the lights on the first-floor landing she noticed a man walking into the library. The man she saw was middle aged with greying hair and a heavy build. He was wearing a black suit with a long jacket. Thinking the man was a stray parent wandering the building she followed him into the library only to find there was no-one there. She later told the *Coventry Evening Telegraph*, 'I have to admit that it spooked me at first and I shot out of the building at a rate of knots. But on reflection there was nothing frightening about it.'

It is not only Singer who haunts the house but also – it is claimed – one of his servants, a nanny's maid called Ermine. Richard Hoare says, 'Ermine, the nanny's maid, allegedly died in 1907 and was buried in the grounds. I have trawled contemporary newspapers and registers of deaths but nothing has ever come up'

Many tales have grown up around Ermine and the whys and wherefores of her death. One story says that there was a birthday party in the house and during a game of hide and seek one child chose to hide in a grandfather clock on the landing. A violent storm raged outside as Ermine searched in vain for the child. As she frantically dashed about, a piercing flash of light while she was on the landing made her stagger backwards and fall over the hallway to her death. Even today the bloodstain in the oak floor is pointed out to those interested.

This is only one story. Another version claims that Ermine was spurned by her sweetheart and threw herself over the balcony. Then, as she was a suicide and couldn't be buried in a churchyard, she was buried within the grounds of Coundon Court. This story is however made up, for suicide burials were allowed in churchyards over fifty years previously. This story may have its origins in the fact that scattered around the grounds of Coundon Court are remains of an ancient building, probably Coundon Chapel. Among these stones which can be found amongst the bushes are some on which old lettering survives. Stones such as these may have been thought to have been a gravestone and possibly given rise to the tale of Ermine's burial in the grounds.

The fact is that there is no evidence yet for the existence of George Singer's lost maid, so we must assume that if not all, then part of her story is a fabrication made up some time in the past to add to the house's already haunted reputation.

The Phantom Coach, Canley

There is more than one version of how the phantom coach of Canley came into being. It is generally said that a stagecoach was passing through the area on Christmas Eve just over 200 years ago when it crashed into a large roadside pond, drowning all its occupants. Another version says that the coach crashed into a swamp and sank, disappearing forever. Afterwards this coach was said to be occasionally seen around the area.

In February 1976 a former Coventry resident, Mrs L.E. Baker of Stratford, wrote to the *Coventry Citizen* saying:

It was a few years before the war. We had been living in Canley Road for a year or two and had been accustomed to cows straying into the front garden. I awoke one night about twelvish and heard horses. I woke my husband and said it sounded as if we had horses in the garden this time.

We both jumped out of bed still hearing the galloping hooves and looked out of the window – and not an animal in sight. I asked my neighbour next morning if she had heard the noise but she hadn't.

A coach such as this is believed to have given rise to the story of Canley's phantom coach

Her remark was that I must have heard the phantom coach and she told me the story, saying it meant trouble. When war was declared not many months after this, this first bombs fell on Coventry.

It was reported in the *Coventry Standard* that another couple saw the coach in 1938 as they drove home from the direction of Berkswell. As they drove along, the husband noticed two lights behind him that looked unusually high. His wife looked around and she could see an old-fashioned coach drawn by four horses. It got nearer and began to bear down upon them and her husband drove faster and faster to try to outrun it, but despite this it began to look as if the coach would hit them. It was quickly decided to pull the car over and let the fast-moving coach pass, which it did, disappearing down the road and leaving the somewhat shocked couple behind. She later told a reporter that she was certain about what they saw and said that she could even see the driver's eyes as the coach passed, saying they were glazed over as if he could not see anything.

The 1930s Phantom Coach pub on the corner of Fletchamstead Highway and Canley Road is said to have later been built on the pond or swamp that the coach crashed into. Subsequently it is said that the coach driver, who they call Charlie, haunts the building. On 15 September 1983 a reporter from the *Coventry Evening Telegraph* spoke to the then landlord of the pub, Hugh Curley, about Charlie. 'Oh him,' he said. 'He takes a stroll round the public bar around one in the morning, turns on the keg cider tap for no apparent reason, talks to Nick, the bar-cellarman, while he's changing a barrel.' 'He even knows my name now', said Nick, who has worked at the pub for fourteen years and appears perfectly sane.

It appears that Hugh had his first meeting with Charlie when he sat up one night doing the books. Suddenly he became aware of someone walking past him. He clearly heard footsteps and the noise of the door being opened and closed again. But he saw nobody and the door never moved. Hugh said, 'My wife was with me at the time and she experienced it too. Strangely enough neither of us was frightened, although whoever it was passed by very close to us.'

A few weeks later when the couple were in bed, Hugh said, 'We heard footsteps on the landing. Somebody came into our bedroom, stood on the far side of the room for a few seconds and then went out. We hadn't been here very long and apparently these things tend to happen when the pub changes hands. It's as though he's giving us a look over.'

There is one problem with Charlie being the coach driver; the Phantom Coach stands on the corner junction of Charter Avenue and Fletchamstead Highway, which is some distance from the main turnpike road. This originally followed the line of the Birmingham Road and Allesley Old Road until the route was improved in the 1830s with the laying of the Holyhead Road. Basically the Phantom Coach doesn't stand on a coaching road and it is extremely unlikely that a coach driver would find himself on a minor lane, which the Canley Road was. So how could Charlie be the coach driver? One would suspect it is purely because of the phantom coach story which covers much of the area. Charlie is more likely to have been perhaps one of the pub's early landlords who has stuck around in the, if you'll excuse the pun, spirit world.

The crisis apparition, Freeman Street

A crisis apparition is different from many other 'general' ghosts for it is usually a vision of a person (usually a close family member) who is in danger or has just recently died. Steve Ball is a member of the Midlands Ghost Research Society and recalls a story of such an apparition told to him many years ago. These are his words:

This is a true story told to me by my Nan, who is no longer with us. If I was to trust anyone it would be my Nan. She was a very level-headed woman and not prone to flights of fancy.

The story happened about thirty-five years ago when my Nan and Granddad lived in Oliver Street, at the back of the old Red House pub. It all started one morning as my Nan was going to have her hair done. She left her house and walked around the corner to get her car out of the garage she had in Freeman Street.

As she reversed out on to the road, she saw a figure in her rear-view mirror standing on the opposite side of the road. She realised it was a man called Mr Airis who owned a fish and chip shop in Freeman Street. Now, Mr Airis had a bit of a reputation. He was well known for keeping people talking. In fact it was a well known fact that if you went into his shop, he would keep you talking that much that your chips would be cold by the time you left.

As my Nan backed out she was faced with a dilemma. She knew Mr Airis had been ill for a few weeks and was stopping at his sister's on the other side of the city. She also knew that if she stopped to see how he was she would miss her appointment. So she decided to carry on and she waved and smiled at Mr Airis as she drove past. He waved back and as she looked in her rear view mirror, she saw him walk towards the entry from Freeman Street to Red House Fields. From the way he was dressed she thought he was on his way to his allotment.

A short time later, as my Nan was having her hair done; a friend came into the shop and asked her if she had heard the news. When my Nan asked what news, she was told that Mr Airis had died the night before at his sister's. It took a while for her to believe this news and when she told them what had happened that morning they understood why.

As I said my Nan was a very level-headed person who stuck by her story, word for word, until she died. She could never understand why she had seen him or why he had shown himself to her. They had known each other for years, but only as acquaintances, rather than close friends.

The haunted jeweller's, Primrose Hill Street

Primrose Hill Street lies in Hillfields, which began life as an extension to Coventry called the 'New Town.' It was laid out from 1828 and housed mainly weavers and watchmakers. One of the first streets to be laid out, it was then on hilly fields noted for their daffodils and primroses. This street led to Primrose Hill House, first mentioned in 1753, originally a private residence and in the late nineteenth century a private boarding school in which the children wore top hats. Nearby was Primrose Hill Park, which lay near to the scene of the murder of Eliza Kington in 1856. It was claimed that this unfortunate, who had her throat slit, haunts this place but no tales survive to the present.

The jeweller's shop in Hillfields shortly before its demolition to make way for a school.

David Betts of Corley Moor does, however, know of another haunting in the vicinity. He recalls:

There used to be a row of old houses in Primrose Hill Street with shops, standing opposite the old cinema, the school is there now. One of these shops was a jeweller's, and one day I stood waiting with other customers to be served in this shop when a clock flew right across the room, from the front window.

The lady who was serving behind the counter could see how shocked we were and said, 'He's at it again! A poltergeist! Since we had a compulsory notice to knock the building down, he has been throwing items around. When I am doing the bookwork in the room upstairs I can feel him walking around me and I say, "Stop doing that, I can't concentrate!"'

The jeweller's moved to Spon Street just before the old shop was demolished to build the school. What happened to our flustered ghost I cannot say.

Tithe Barn ghost, Allesley Old Road

At the top of the Allesley Old Road once stood a toll house with two white gates, one of which gave entrance to the Allesley Old Road and the other the Holyhead Road. Behind the toll house once stood a large ancient barn, known locally as the 'Tithe Barn' possibly because it was used to collect Allesley Church's tithes of corn, etc. In the mid-nineteenth century a farmhand is said to have hanged himself in the barn and because he was a suicide was buried in the road before the toll house.

The farmhand was said to haunt both the road and the barn before it was all demolished for road widening in around 1931.

The Allesley toll gate with the Tithe Barn behind, said to have been haunted by a suicide.

The highwayman, Westwood Heath

In the early hours of a December morning in 1986 a young woman left her friend's house in Westwood Heath to drive home into Coventry. That morning she saw something she could not explain. As she was about to set off home she noticed set back in the shadows cast from the street lamp the motionless figure of a man on horseback.

The figure was only a few yards away and as she looked she couldn't see his face, for the man wore a long black cloak with a brimmed hat pulled around his face, giving him all the appearance of a highwayman. What she had seen didn't register at first; she then stopped and looked back again only to see that the man and horse were gone.

'When I looked back again there was just nobody there,' she said, 'My family reckon I must have been dreaming, but I was wide awake and I hadn't been drinking. I know what I saw.'

Nailcote House, Tile Hill

Nailcote House, an Elizabethan timbered building just beyond Tile Hill, has a reputation for being haunted. In the past, rumours have circulated in the area of hauntings and a mysterious murder taking place there. The owners of the ivy-clad hall in 1938 were Mr and Mrs McFarlane. They confirmed the stories, telling the press that mysterious things began to happen the moment they moved in. Mrs McFarlane said, 'I did not believe any of the stories that were told when we took the house. But that there is something strange and uncanny about it I am convinced.'

One of the haunted parts of the building was said to be the secret passage leading from the dining room to a secret room on the top floor. A moveable oak panel in the inglenook fireplace is the only known access to the secret passage. It is said that this passageway was constructed by 'Little John', who during the latter part of the sixteenth century created many secret hiding places and priest holes in Midland houses.

It was always said that dark strange sounds came from the hall's secret passage and it was so on the McFarlane's first night when weird sounds from it kept the family up all night. The following morning they discovered a pair of owls had found their way into the passage and were desperately trying to escape.

Shortly after this Mrs McFarlane said, 'We were seated in the dining room one evening when suddenly I heard the front door open and then close again. My husband immediately got up and went to see who was there, but could not see anyone. The remarkable thing about it was that the door had only a few minutes earlier been locked and barred. We were talking about this a few minutes later and trying to find some explanation for it when we both heard the door open and close again. As the door closed, we heard the glass in one of the panels rattle as it always does.

'My husband rushed out… I heard him unlock the door and go out. Outside the dog was barking in a most unusual way. He continued to bark for some time, during which my husband searched all around the garden, without discovering anything. Just as he was about to return, however, a friend who was visiting us walked up the drive and the first thing she commented on was that a strange-looking man dressed in black had hurried past her in the drive.'

Things got worse and Mrs McFarlane told the press, 'It became so bad that none of us would stop alone in the house. Eventually it so upset my daughter that she became really ill and had to be sent away, and when one of my sons returned after having been away from home for some time, he tried to persuade me to give the house up.'

Mrs McFarlane then said that the house was thought to be haunted by the ghost of a former butler. Locals added that around 1840 one of the grooms stabbed the butler in the back, killing him instantly. The murder was said to have taken place in the barn near the hall's entrance.

It was said that those who occupied a particular bedroom could be woken in the middle of the night by an unseen hand opening the door or throwing things off the dressing table onto the floor. One regular user of the room was said to always place the contents of the dressing table onto the floor before retiring.

Another interesting feature of the house was an underground tunnel which led from the cellar over several hundred yards to Nailcote Hall. Legend has it that Oliver Cromwell walked this tunnel which has long since been bricked up.

The Pirate's Grave

The church of Mary Magdalene in Wyken with its stumpy tower is considered the oldest in Coventry. In the churchyard once stood a gravestone carved with a skull with deeply recessed eye sockets and crossbones. This it was known to all and sundry as the 'Pirate's Grave'. Sometime in the nineteenth century a rumour spread amongst local children that if you chanted and walked three times around the stone the ghost of the pirate buried there would be raised and appear before you.

This led to a regular procession of terrified youngsters running screaming from the churchyard at night convinced the pirate had appeared before them. This continued and by the twentieth century the eye sockets of the skull had grown because of numerous youngsters pushing their fingers into them. By the 1960s the process had changed slightly and to summon the ghost one had to walk three times around the stone and throw a stone through the church window. Not surprisingly the vicar quickly picked up on this, initially driving the children away, but soon he decided to have the stone removed before all of the church windows were smashed.

Why a pirate would be buried at Wyken I do not know, but what I do know is that the skull and crossbones were common symbols of mortality, not necessarily piracy, and appeared regularly on graves from the sixteenth century onwards.

An early eighteenth-century gravestone like the one which stood in Wyken churchyard referred to as the 'Pirate's Grave'.

Walsgrave's haunted house

Up until the 1960s on the site of the present Beckbury Road stood a 400-year-old house set within 10 acres of landscaped gardens called 'The Kennels'. This was once home to the Verrall sisters. Miss Florence and Miss Nee were archetypal Edwardian ladies even up to their deaths in 1953. Both ladies were an integral part of village life in Walsgrave and Miss Nee was involved in country pursuits and horses while Miss Florence organised tea parties and was the leading light at St Mary's Church.

Both ladies expected to be treated as such. In 1986, the late Reg Johnson recalled 'Miss Florence stopping me once and saying, "Johnson, why don't you raise your hat to a lady, your father always did" – but I never did. She was that type of person, you see.'

Miss Florence died at The Kennels aged ninety-two in 1953, quickly followed eight months later by her sister Miss Nee who was eighty-eight. The two dutiful unmarried sisters' deaths meant the end of an era at their beloved 'Kennels' and in the village of Walsgrave.

The Kennels was sold on and the new occupants soon began to notice doors opening and closing on their own and strange limping footsteps were heard around the building. Eventually the culprit was seen, the ghost of an old lady wearing a frilly nightgown and nightcap and walking with a limp.

A priest was called in to perform an exorcism but it proved ineffective. Then a medium was brought in who seemed to quieten the old lady down for a short time. In the 1960s caravans were placed in the grounds and when some labourers slept in the old house it is said they always insisted a priest was present.

Soon after a new family moved into the house, they got used to the nocturnal wanderings and it is said the old lady became part of the family, although few guests stayed twice as a result of her presence. Interestingly the ghost got more active if some change was afoot in the village.

Who was this ghost? The answer is easy; one of the Verrall sisters had a club foot and therefore had a slight limp. Which one I don't know but both sisters would not have wanted to leave each other or their lovely home and they certainly didn't want to leave the village which was close to both their hearts. Maybe they are still watching over it!

The armoured spectre, Allesley

On the Birmingham road in Allesley village stands a fine old stone building appropriately named the 'Stone House'. The old pathway that runs next to the Stone House was said to have been the entrance to the long-gone Allesley Castle. It is said that over the centuries passers-by had seen a man in armour standing by or walking along this pathway, before disappearing into thin air.

Dr John Orton, who lived in Allesley Hall in the 1930s, had a scrapbook in which was found the following:

In the turbulent days of King Stephen in 1146, 'Black Roger,' the Baron of Maxstoke, incensed that he could not marry the daughter of Sir Fulk Hastings, attacked Allesley Castle, slaughtering the occupants and burning it to the ground. Will Braynes, the seneschal, is said to have escaped,

Two children walk down the pathway said to have originally led to Allesley Castle and haunted by an armoured ghost. The Stone House is on the right.

but was pursued and eventually murdered near the Pack-Horse Gatehouse of the castle. The Old Stone House on the Birmingham road is reputed to be a remnant of that gatehouse and tales were told of a man in armour who haunts the site.

History tells us nothing of 'Black Roger' although the manor of Allesley appears to have come into the hands of the Hastings family in the 1260s or '70s. The Hastings, who also owned Fillongley Castle, built a residence here which had a deer park stretching over to the present Broad Lane.

This spiritually busy little lane is also said to be haunted by a grey lady, a phantom coach and a headless horseman.

THREE

HAUNTED PUBS

The Radford ghosts, Radford Road

The once-popular Radford Hotel was closed at the beginning of the twenty-first century and suffered constant vandalism before it was prematurely demolished in 2002; the land has since been built upon. The building was one of the last large nineteenth-century buildings left in Radford and began life as the handsome private residence of David Spencer, a silk weaving manufacturer in 1830. In the early part of the reign of Queen Victoria it was converted into a Catholic school with its own chapel. Later the house again became a private residence and was sold to the De Creese family who in 1900 sold it on to the Pughs in what was then still semi-rural Radford.

The head of the house was the notable Vernon Pugh, managing director of the Rudge Whitworth Cycle Company. His son Dickie was a personal friend of the Duke of Kent, who stayed many times at the house when he was in the area. The house and its beautiful grounds were also home to many local events, such a fêtes and cricket matches.

Its glory days passed, in 1929 Radford House was sold to Atkinson's Brewery, who sold it on to Mitchell & Butlers, and the building was renamed the Radford Hotel. No early stories appear to have filtered out from the house about anything strange happening when it was a private residence. It was only when it became a pub that the stories emerged about it being haunted.

One ex-landlady, Sue Freemantle, remembers it well. She says, 'From 1981 to 1990 my husband and I were licensees of the Radford Hotel. It had quite a history and plenty of ghostly goings on. The two most talked about by the locals concerned the function room and the ghostly nanny. The function room, when the Radford was a private house, was a private chapel. Every so often a cross would appear on the wall. Being a logical person, the time of day, plus weather conditions, such as the sun, it could be explained away. But one night, when the lights were out I did see it, a shimmering cross which faded away in seconds.'

As for the nanny, Sue recalls, 'I was told she was looking for two children who had died in a fire and strange as it seems the haunting was in the middle ladies' toilet in the lounge. There was every so often a cold spot, and ladies using the toilet often heard whispering, but no-one was there. Some thought their friends were playing tricks upon them, banging on the toilet door and even humming hymns.'

Radford House as it was around 1920. The building was allegedly haunted. (Coventry City Libraries)

'One lady who was not a regular and claimed to be a medium phoned me constantly to ask if she could do a séance. She had used the toilet and was convinced there was a lady trying to reach her. However, I declined the offer. We also had a German Shepherd who for some unknown reason would stand in the lounge when it was empty, fix his eyes on the ladies' toilet and growl and bark.'

There was also another apparition. Sue continues, 'However, the weirdest one was what Ron my husband experienced just before we left. He used to say the only spirits were the ones we sold behind the bar. He believed that such a big old building had lots of atmosphere and that noises and cold spots could be explained. Anyway the staff had gone, it was about 11.30 p.m., I was upstairs and Ron and the last customer were in the lounge. Ken the customer was about to go when he asked Ron if there was anything behind him as the hairs on the back of his neck were standing up. Ron saw behind Ken, by one of the square pillars, a figure, cloaked and with a cowl covering his head. It was only for a second but it scared them both. It unnerved him so much that he phoned me upstairs to come and lock up!'

The *Coventry Evening Telegraph* reported some incidents in August 1984 when Sue and Ron were there. Barman Allan Parker said he with others caught a glimpse of the woman who haunted the toilet area as he sat talking to other members of staff. He told a reporter, 'We saw the face of an old woman in a white veil and it was peering through the window in the door of the ladies'. One girl fainted but when the rest of us investigated there was nobody in there.'

Former cleaner in the pub Hilda Thornett also told the reporter that she had seen a shadow cross the window in the toilet, felt a cold presence brush past her as she cleaned the stairs and had also seen the shimmering cross on the wall in the function room.

So the Radford appears to have had two ghosts, the old 'nanny' who strangely appears to be wearing a white veil, assuming it was a veil and not how the face looked, and a cloaked, cowled figure. Oral tradition says that the nanny was searching for two children while a fire was in progress and they all died, probably in the area which was then occupied by the ladies' toilets. Maybe one day the truth behind this event may come to light. Oral history also places the shimmering cross in the chapel and indeed when the building was a Catholic school it did have a chapel. The story however says that the chapel was there when it was a private house, this may be so for the De Creese family may have been Catholics and to have their own chapel within the house may have been the incentive to acquire it. That said it may also be a piece of mixed up history.

I'll let ex-landlady of the 'Radford' Sue Freemantle have the final word: 'The Radford is now gone, a sad end for such a grand building. It would be nice to know that some of its ghostly tales were recorded.'

The White Lion ghost

The White Lion pub in Brownshill Green began life as an ordinary Victorian cottage which later had an off-licence added. Later it became a popular rural pub. In 1984 the then pub landlord Len Firth said, 'There was the time late one night when the doorbell rang. I went downstairs in the dark to answer it and as I opened the door all the lights went on in the room. The light switch was across the other side of the room and there was nobody on the doorstep.'

This incident only happened once but other incidents occur regularly, such as the vacuum cleaner being moved into the centre of the floor by unseen hands and bottles moving on their own.

The Golden Cross ghost, city centre

The timbered Golden Cross pub which stands on the corner of Hay and Pepper Lane is traditionally said to have been built upon the site of Coventry's fifteenth-century mint which produced a number of gold and silver coins of King Edward IV. The pub is thought to date from the fifteenth and sixteenth centuries and received major restoration in the late nineteenth century using timbers from the bell frame of St Michael.

Maurice Burnell's late wife worked at the pub in the 1970s, so Maurice has some memories concerning the pub's ghost. He says, 'Mary Spicer who was the chef at the pub told me that one night after closing, Trevor Johnson who was the manager placed one of the till drawers under the bar counter and as he was taking the other till drawer up the stairs, the till under the bar shot out and all the money was thrown all over the floor. Mary said the ghost is of a sea captain who died in the pub. My late wife Gloria saw the ghost and gave a vivid description of him as being dressed in those thigh-long boots, which made me think he was a cavalier.' According to Maurice other members of staff also saw or felt the presence of the ghost, which they believed was a sea captain who died in the pub. He was recently told that things also happened in the cellar such as objects being thrown through the air, also a banging on a dividing door. Many of the pub's female staff are reluctant to go in the cellar. The present staff at the Cross, tell me that they believe it is haunted by four ghosts, including an "old man" in the upstairs front room.'

The late Gloria Burnell outside the Golden Cross where she saw the sea captain/cavalier ghost.

The recently demolished Smithfield Hotel in Hales Street.

The Smithfield Hotel, Hales Street

The Tudor-style Smithfield Hotel built originally by the side of the old Smithfield cattle market was only knocked down in 2000 as part of the Phoenix Initiative. The pub was a popular venue and boarding house for the many celebrities who played at the Coventry Hippodrome which stood until recently opposite.

The pub was said to have been haunted by the stage, screen and television personality Peter Butterworth who died in one of the bedrooms while appearing at the Hippodrome.

The Dyers Arms, Spon End

The Dyers Arms in Spon End was reported as being haunted in 1988 when it was said that the popular pub was full of strange and unexplained happenings. The landlady at the time was Mavis Ogden, who told the *Coventry Evening Telegraph* that their Alsatian 'Storm' was afraid of nothing except going down into the pub cellar, which he would flatly refuse. Mavis believed much of the odd happenings in the pub were focused in the cellar.

The Dyers Arms, a nineteenth-century pub haunted by an ex-landlord who died in the cellar.

Barrie Ogden the landlord said he lost count of the amount of times that he had found the cellar in disarray, with coolers and pumps turned off and plugs pulled out of sockets. Barrie told reporter Peter Walters, that he had a frightening experience some months previously while working in the cellar at 6.30 in the morning. As he stood by the sink a box which had been on the cellar steps behind him flew past his head and hit the wall next to him. Barrie spun around expecting someone there, only to see an empty space.

Another who experienced an unusual event in the cellar was a barman who was alone in the pub, when he was suddenly aware of the sound of barrels being moved about in the cellar. He went down to find no-one there, and was so unnerved he spent the rest of the afternoon sitting outside on the doorstep.

Mavis had a similar experience. She said, 'I was on my own sweeping the floor in the bar, when I heard what sounded like buckets being clanged together in the cellar. I didn't investigate, I just fled.'

Another part of the pub has seen incidents. In 1982 a cleaner was working in a back room when suddenly her apron was ripped off spinning her around with the force, but nobody was there! Seeing the room was empty, she crossed herself and walked out never to return again.

Another incident involved the men's toilets. In 1987 a local rugby player was celebrating with friends when something happened. He walked out of the gent's as white as a sheet and a few minutes later informed his friends what he had seen. He said he had a feeling someone was watching him and on turning around saw a little girl in a white dress standing staring at him; as he stared back in surprise the child vanished. Mavis believed there was an explanation for this, saying that a story had been passed down of an ex-landlord losing his four-year-old daughter while here.

Another incident happened shortly before the interview when a barmaid sitting at the bar saw a man in the semi-darkness of the lounge. A search was made of the building but as usual nothing was found.

The fact that noises are often in heard in the pub's cellar may give us a clue to the origin of this haunting. The *Coventry Standard* of 8 August 1856 states that:

On Saturday morning last an inquest was held at the Dyer's Arms, Spon-street … on view was the body of Edward Walmsley, aged forty-five years, the landlord of the above house, who was found dead in his own cellar about nine o'clock of Thursday night.

The first witness was John Gillings, a dyer who said that Walmsley had been called down the cellar to tap a new barrel. He had been gone some time and his wife asked John Chaplin to go down the cellar and check that her husband was alright. Gillings said, 'I was called out by Mrs Walmsley to go into the cellar to look for the deceased, whom I found upon his face, about 4ft from the cellar steps, and near to the barrel; he had gone down to tap a barrel; myself and two or three others got him up the steps into the yard; he appeared quite dead.

Fredrick Barton a surgeon told the inquest that when he arrived Walmsley was in the yard, 'quite dead, no treatment or application would have been of any use; he had the appearance of a man who had died from suffocation by the inhalation of carbonic acid gas.'

Walmsley had indeed died from gas inhalation; when tests were done with a candle it ceased to burn three feet from the cellar floor. Walmsley knew of the dangers of this gas given off during the fermentation process and had asked the council permission to let a ventilation grill into the street. This was refused and Edward Walmsley paid for this with his life. Edward Walmsley was described as a man of modest manners, remarkably generous and kindly. He was also noted as being something of an artist and collector of art.

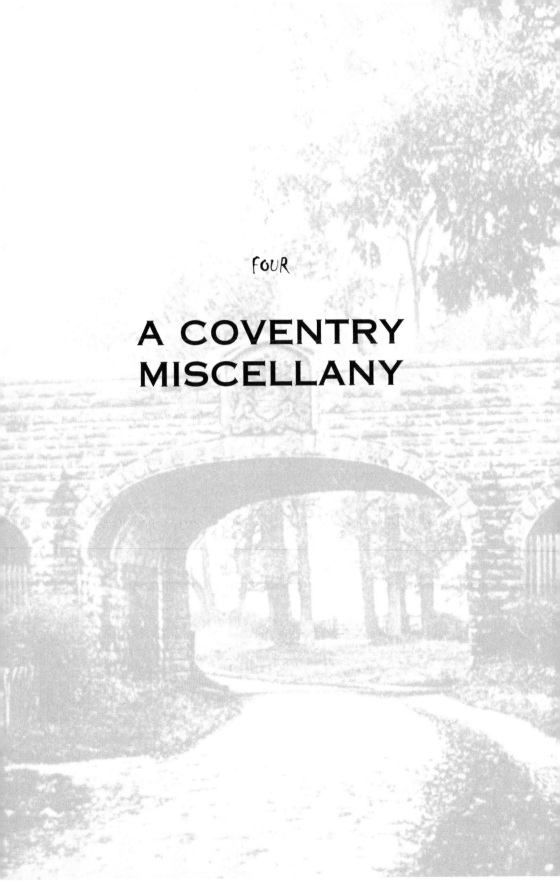

FOUR

A COVENTRY
MISCELLANY

There are many reports of hauntings in the city for which are only brief references to incidents or for which there are few details. I have listed them here so they are not forgotten.

Swanswell Gate. The City Ambassadors who currently occupy this ancient city gate say that they often experience the feeling of not being alone here and things have actually been thrown across the room.

The Lyric Cinema. The former cinema stands in Holbrook Lane. Former employee Ron Severs recalls one or two unusual events at the cinema. Apparently a former projectionist haunted the projection room and one day Ron was carrying an armful of film reels to the room when the heavy metal door that he was just wondering how to open suddenly swung open unaided. Not surprisingly he dropped the reels in surprise. One day all the staff were in the manager's office when the internal phone rang from the projection room. It was answered and of course no-one was there.

When the same thing happened on another occasion three members of staff converged simultaneously on the room again to find it empty. On another occasion after the cinema was locked and Ron was walking past a nearby house the lady of the house said, 'You're opening early these days!' Ron asked her what she meant and she told him she had seen someone waving to her from the projection room. Ron knew this couldn't be so because at the time the building was locked and empty.

The Forum Cinema. The old Forum Cinema, now a bowling alley, was said to be haunted by a policeman who had been seen on a number of occasions in a small room to the left of the cinema's staircase.

Whitley Mill, Whitley. The last occupant of the mill before it was demolished says that footsteps would often be heard coming down the stairs and the family collie would snarl as it looked towards the stairs, from which no-one descended.

Keresley Heath. The triangular heath known to locals as the 'common' was said in the nineteenth century to be haunted by a small boy who drowned in a flooded pit which could once be found there.

Whitley Mill, c. 1905.

Woodway Lane, Walsgrave/Potter's Green. Once along Woodway Lane could be found the 'Gypsy Pit'. It was said that in the nineteenth century a little gypsy girl drowned here. It was claimed that if you jumped on the large stone by the pit three times the ghost of the gypsy girl would appear.

Coventry Transport Museum. It is said that someone once saw a ghost believed to be Horace Wilton Bartleet sitting on a cycle in the museum. Horace Bartleet was an avid collector of cycles and cycle memorabilia and left his collection to the city. He is said to have died while on a cycle, maybe the one in the museum.

The Herbert, Jordan Well. One evening after closing members of staff saw someone waving through the window at them. They did not recognise the person but assumed that they had somehow locked someone inside. A thorough search was made of the building and no-one was found.

Dunlop Aviation, Swallow Drive, Whitmore Park. Many years ago in one section of the factory an old coat hung on a coathanger. No-one would touch this coat for it was believed to belong to an ex-employee who was said to haunt the factory.

Kingfisher Gallery, Spon Street. The owner of this fine old shop says that strange noises such as groans and moans are sometimes heard coming from below the shop. One would look to the cellar if the shop had one, but the owner says that if there is one he doesn't know of it. The fact that the shop was built over the city ditch though supports this possibility. There is also a shadow sometimes seen in the shop and a feeling of being watched, and the owner believes this to be a Victorian lady.

Coat of Arms Bridge Road, the scene of a haunting. It has changed little since this photograph was taken around 1910.

Cathedral Lanes. It is claimed by some that odd things are seen and heard in this modern shopping mall in the heart of Broadgate. This is not, perhaps, that surprising considering the old Coventry Gaol stood on the rear of the site and there are still graves there of prisoners who died in the gaol, including Mary Ball who was hanged there in 1849.

Kenilworth Road. Well-known cartoonist Heritage Peters died in 1965, and stipulated that after his death his favourite three-legged 'sentry chair' should remain in his house. He warned that if anyone sold his chair, removing it from the house, he would come back and haunt them. Whether he was joking or not later occupants didn't want to put to the test, for the chair remained in the house until at least 1988.

Coat of Arms Bridge Road. Stories circulate that people driving along this road sometimes see a young woman run out in front of their cars. On investigation nothing is ever found.

Walsgrave Hospital. Reports have come from certain wards in the hospital for many years of sightings of a nun. Even in the 1980s I was asked if a nunnery lay on this site and replied in the negative. Perhaps the many nun sightings in the hospital are down to a now deceased sister who visited sick patients there soon after the hospital was built. Strangely a recent sighting describes another figure watching over the sick; a woman with a shining cross on her forehead!

FIVE

FURTHER AFIELD, BUT NOT TOO FAR!

The haunted house

In the Brownshill Green/Corley area stands a house which once had something of a reputation. Interviewed in the 1950s Peter Tooth who owned the house told the press, 'When we first went into the house undoubtedly there was something radically wrong there. No-one from the village would go up the drive and past the house till we moved in. They said they wouldn't go past for a £5 note. We didn't know it was haunted when we moved in. Houses weren't to be got in those days so we had to stick it. It was very nervy at first.'

Peter told of what happened, 'We used to hear chains drawn down the drive. We could hear them rattling and grating on the ground. Then when we were in the kitchen we used to hear a noise like something rolling down the banister and stairs. In the village they used to call that the "Barrel of Beer". My wife thought it sounded more like a motorbike.

'We used to hear the noises two or three times a week when we first moved in. Then they wore off. But we've seen doors open and there's no-one there and heard footsteps on the landing. All the rows came from above; there was never anything in the cellar or on the ground floor.

'Nobody before us stopped in the house very long,' Peter said. 'It must have been the noises that drove them away. There was more row than what you saw. If we could have seen what it was, I could have had a go at it.'

Mrs Tooth told the reporter that she had seen a man coming down the stairs in a nightshirt and holding a candle in his hand and Peter Tooth added that he had also seen something, saying, 'It was when we first went to look at the house. We were going down the field with the farmer and in the gateway I saw a form. It was a woman in black. I was going to point her out to the farmer and my wife, but it disappeared, I never saw it again.'

Their son-in-law who lived at the house for a while said he saw a woman dressed in white, with a covering like a nun, her head bowed and hands held together as though in prayer. Peter Tooth suggested the origin of the hauntings: 'There was talk about a man being murdered there years ago by the fireplace in the front room.'

Another oddity about the house came up when the attic floor was being demolished; workmen noted that chains were fitted to the wall and the doorway was barred, 'like a police station,' one workman said. The strange room was demolished making the cottage one storey lower and hopefully a little quieter.

Mr Tooth and Mr Ward examine one of the chains in the attic.

The ghosts of Coombe Abbey

Coombe Abbey lies off the Brinklow Road on the edge of Coventry. It has a long history as a monastic house then private house and now a hotel with extensive grounds used for recreation by the people of Coventry and beyond. Coombe also has many ghosts, starting with the monks.

Coombe's best-known ghost is known to all as Henry. Henry is thought to be Abbot Geoffrey who was murdered here in 1345. Generally all sightings of monks on the site are put down to Abbot Geoffrey. One night many years ago the head ranger's wife saw Henry crossing the courtyard by the cloister. Interestingly the bottom of the figure was below ground level, as it walked along on the original medieval level.

Henry is generally the one blamed for much glass-smashing which took place in the now gone courtyard bar opened in the 1970s. It was not unusual for staff to find smashed glass when opening the bar in the morning despite, the fact that the doors were locked and the windows impossibly small for a person to get through.

Henry continued smashing things in later bars and in the banqueting kitchen. When responding to news of the abbey being made into a hotel, Lois Pargetor interviewed in 1991 said of Henry, 'I think he will cause a bit of disturbance. Things will start to happen and he may throw things around a bit.' Lois, who had at that time worked at Coombe for twenty years added, 'Girls have been working behind the bar and glasses have gone flying across the cloister by themselves.'

The new hotel did indeed open with Henry putting in the odd appearance, as he still does. However, Henry is not the only ghost, for in the past a number of people have heard light footsteps hurrying across the courtyard. Those who heard them think it sounded as if a young girl was crossing the court.

She may be Matilda, who is said to haunt the stable block. Matilda, legend has it, was a green-eyed gypsy girl who was made pregnant by the master of the house in the late seventeenth century. Matilda, it is said, informed her master of her situation and was subsequently cast out. The trauma caused her to gave birth to a stillborn child and she swore revenge, calling down a curse on the family that every first born would die tragically before reaching middle age.

Above: *Coombe Abbey as it looked, minus its church, in the late sixteenth century. The courtyard in front is where the monk was seen and the footsteps are heard.*

Left: *A medieval monk.*

William, 1st Earl of Craven.

The family in question was the Craven family who acquired Coombe from Sir John Harington in the seventeenth century. The family held the estate until the 1920s and interestingly many of the male line have indeed died young under tragic circumstances, including some of its more recent male members.

Just down the road from Coombe in a bend in the road still stands an old lodge gate. Here it is said people have seen a spectral horseman. Some have noted how at this point no matter what the weather the temperature always drops. Another rider of a different type was seen one evening in 1975. While Bud Brooker was driving from Brinklow past Coombe the sun was going down and the evening was pleasant and on the road before him was one lone cyclist.

As he approached the cyclist he began to realise there was something different about her. She was riding a sit-up-and-beg cycle and dressed in a long brown dress, black boots and a hat tied with a cream coloured veil under the chin. Mr Brooker was intrigued and assumed she was in fancy dress or in a rally. As he began to overtake and pulled up alongside her he took another look only to find that she had vanished. He looked behind; there was no turn off, and no-one there, the lady on the cycle had vanished into thin air.

The Grey Lady, Baginton

The village of Baginton on the edge of Coventry has a long history and a number of ghosts, the best known being the Grey Lady. It is said that as long as anyone can remember a lady has been seen to glide through the churchyard and across the lane and into the old rectory. She is described as almost transparent and wearing a long grey gown. The owner of Baginton Rectory in 1980 was a Dr Glasgow; he heard about the ghost as soon as he moved in around 1963 when a local farmer told him of the Grey Lady and said that when he visited the rectory at night his dog always refused to enter. The good doctor and his wife kept an open mind on the ghost but never actually saw it themselves.

In December 1984 a previous owner of the rectory, John Sheffield, wrote to the *Coventry Evening Telegraph* telling of what he knew of the Grey Lady of Baginton. He wrote:

My family lived in Baginton Rectory from 1949 to 1960 and during that time had many experiences with the so-called Grey Lady. Legend has it that she was a servant girl at the original Baginton Hall. She had a sweetheart at the then 'Big House' near the church. We believe that the 'Big House' was a farmhouse named after the then owners, the Underhill's. It became a rectory in 1628 through a benefices transfer.

We found the first reference to the apparition in the tithe barn, now a beautiful house. On the inside of the stable door was the reference: 'Beware of the Grey Lady'. I thought in those early days that the legend was untrue, but I was (as was my family) often put to the test.'

I well remember being told by a Mr Poole who lived on Coventry Road of his seeing the 'lady' walking back from the rectory, through the churchyard, and along the path that would have led from and to the hall.

My late father-in-law, a most level-headed man, told us of the time when he and his wife were staying at the rectory. My wife and I were out and around ten o'clock, when all was dark and still, he looked up from his chair by the fire and gazed out of the uncurtained window giving a view on the drive.

He saw someone apparently crossing the lawn. Thinking it was one of us returning he went into the front lobby, switched on the outside light, opened the front door and was amazed to find nothing there. There was a distinct odour of perfume such as musk.

On another occasion, my late mother-in-law was in the kitchen making an early morning cup of tea. She assured us that the door to the stairs opened and that she felt the presence of someone. As she turned to look towards the door the apparition vanished, but again there was the faint odour of musk.

As for me, I also experienced her presence as she glided through the house to the main bedrooms … she was – and maybe still is – a friendly ghost, who still manifests herself to those in love.

Another grey lady of a much more frightening nature was recorded by Peter Walters in his *Coventry Evening Telegraph* booklet 'Ghosts and Legends of Coventry and Warwickshire'. He reports that on a chilly, foggy November night in 1984 Mark Batchelor and his girlfriend Sonia Nash were driving home from a quiet evening in a country pub. The couple went through Baginton and turned slowly into Rowley Road as the fog was still cloaking the way, when suddenly the car headlights picked out a woman standing by the side of the road. No ordinary woman this but wearing a long white gown with a ruffled collar.

Above: *The Grey Lady is said to be seen gliding from the church to the rectory.*

Left: *A classic grey lady, but perhaps not as unpleasant as the Rowley Road grey lady.*

As they drew nearer to the figure they could see that she was middle-aged and unusually tall with a grey face and black matted hair tied into a knot. Mark said, 'She wasn't moving, just staring intently straight at us. In the light her eyes appeared to be very green and piercing.' When they reached the figure it suddenly turned and pointed towards the direction of Coventry Airport, then swung around and pointed back towards the Lunt. 'It was as if she was trying to tell us something,' Mark recalled.

Mark returned to the spot on a number of occasions to try to find an explanation for what he had seen, but nothing. He said, 'I've wondered many times whether it wasn't a real person... But the clothes were very weird and I've never seen anybody who looked like that. The colour of her face was unreal, indescribable really. I should have stopped and investigated, but I didn't have it in me at the time. I was in a terrible state when I got home.'

Whether this ghost and the rectory ghost are one and the same it is hard to tell. It seems unlikely as the rectory is about half a mile away and the Rowley Road ghost appears to be of a more frightening nature. Why she was standing at the roadside is unknown, the road isn't ancient, but appears to be a later possible field enclosure road of the eighteenth or nineteenth century. One possibility of course is always the roadside suicide burial as other roadside ghosts around the land have been seen near the site of such burials.

These are not Baginton's only ghosts, for the old castle site near the river Sowe is also said to be haunted. When the site of the castle was excavated in 1934 apparently a local warned the diggers to be careful as they might disturb the spirit of the headless lady who was said to haunt the ruins. Local tradition has it that she was a beautiful young lady who was foully murdered or executed when the castle was still standing and in the hands of Sir William Bagot, member of the Privy Council of King Richard II. Near to the castle ruins stands an unusual square stone

Baginton Hall as it was.

building; no-one knew what it was, one story claims it was used as a prison and another says it was used by quoits players. The building and its surrounds are said to be haunted by a quoits player who is said to have thrown his quoit so hard that it overshot and rolled down the bank towards the river. The player is said to have pursued it, stumbled and broke his neck and ever since haunted the place of his last game.

Baginton Hall itself – now gone – was built to replace the castle and it suffered a dreadful fire in 1706. The hall was rebuilt and completed in 1714. This second hall also suffered a fire on 7 October 1889 when the butler was refilling oil lamps. The hall thereafter stood empty but despite this in 1899 the alarm was raised once again that the hall was in flames. Crowds turned up but nothing was amiss. This happened again years later when the wings had been restored. Three men passed it and one shouted out that the hall was on fire; the other two men however gradually calmed their friend down and showed him that, as in 1899, there was no real fire. Just his imagination – or was it?

The phantom lorry, Ryton

The London Road passing by Knightlow Hill was in the recent past still a single-carriageway with a reputation of being dangerous, for the unusual reason that it was haunted by a phantom lorry. A story is told that in the mid-1930s a shaken driver told of a lorry which drove straight at him and as he desperately tried to avoid crashing into it the lorry went straight through his car. As it passed through the terrified driver was fixed in the gaze of the grinning white-faced driver in the lorry cab.

Many accidents on this stretch of road were dealt with by PC George Forsythe and time after time drivers told him that they were forced off the road by a lorry which came straight at them with lights blazing. This terrifying event ended just on impact as the vehicle simply disappeared and the oncoming vehicle careered off the road.

PC Forsythe often put the event down to too much drinking in the local hostelry. That was until one day something happened to make him change his mind. On a winter's night in 1952 he was heading home down Knightlow Hill in thick fog and heavy snow, when suddenly he heard the sound of a heavy lorry skidding and rolling over. As he ran to the scene a car appeared and crashed into the lorry, followed by another, then another, then another.

Visibility was zero and more vehicles were in danger of ramming into the mass of tangled vehicles and PC Forsythe quickly gathered the uninjured and got them to gather branches from the hedgerow and built bonfires 100 yards either side of the crash, to warn those approaching. As PC Forsythe was about to deal with the injured someone shouted 'Here's another one coming!'

He stood and watched as out of the fog and snow appeared bearing down on him at speed an old-fashioned lorry with a tarpaulin-covered back. The driver seemed unaware of the fires and PC Forsythe desperately tried to wave it down. Despite this it roared past, passing between him and one of the bonfires and PC Forsythe became immediately aware that he could see the fire straight through the lorry.

Despite this his senses told him to expect the vehicle to impact into the crashed vehicles and he ran after it, expecting any moment to hear a loud crash. No such thing happened and as PC Forsythe came into view of the crashed vehicles he quickly realised that the speeding lorry had in fact disappeared into thin air.

*George Forsythe in 1975 when head of Coventry subdivision. (*Coventry Evening Telegraph*)*

PC Forsythe later became a senior officer in the Coventry Police and in October 1984, after his retirement, was asked about the event. 'There had been local talk before of a phantom lorry on the road,' he said, 'but I had always dismissed the stories out of hand. That night I'm convinced I saw it.'

Five days after George Forsythe said the above, E. Brookes of Dorchester Way, Walsgrave wrote to the *Telegraph* with a possible explanation:

> As a boy of five years I lived with my family in a bungalow on the London Road, Stretton-on-Dunsmore. Our home was situated about 200 yards along the road from an old farmhouse-cum-transport cafe … now the site of Bob's Café.
>
> My father used to cycle morning and night to and from his place of work … I remember him getting home late one night during the winter of 1926-27 and telling us of a lorry that had crashed on Knightlow Hill, the driver being trapped in his cab and burned to death. I wonder, could this be George Forsythe's phantom.
>
> My memory of lorries in those days was steaming monsters with solid tyres that could be heard from quite a distance. More so if the tyres had been cut and damaged. The clip, clip, clip, on the road was more frightening than any claxon or wind horn.

Ghostly monks, Fillongley

The village of Fillongley lies a short distance from Coventry. Its church is dedicated to St Mary and contains one or two things of interest, including a number of spirits. Early in the twentieth century reports were made that people had seen monks in the church and heard chanting. Some claimed that when they walked down the path to the building sometimes it felt as if an unseen presence was trying to hold them back.

It is said that during the Second World War the vicar's wife went into the church just as it was getting dark and was surprised to see movement. She saw a monk in a black habit standing before the altar. Despite the fact that she had just left her husband at home, seeing a man dressed thus told her it must be him and she called out his name. As she did so the figure faded away, leaving the vicar's wife stunned.

A story is told of when the hauntings were at their height and a clergyman went in to exorcise the ghostly monks. It is said that as he called out the order in Latin he was suddenly aware that he was getting the appropriate Latin responses from disembodied voices. The monks were joining in the service which was supposed to exorcise them. Not surprisingly the clergy quickly left.

The haunting continued, for in 1991 sixteen-year-old church organist Simon Tayton was practising in the church one night. After he had finished he was just going to lock up when he saw a monk praying in the front pew. Knowing the stories and not stopping to ask questions he fled the building and headed straight for the warden's house.

According to the *Coventry Evening Telegraph* Simon said, 'I was only ten yards from it. I noticed a faint brown-white glow coming from the figure. It freaked me out. The warden couldn't believe how pale I was. I was absolutely terrified.'

It is said that the church's altar stone came from Maxstoke Priory and people have assumed that the monks came with it. The Maxstoke order had a bit of a reputation, not for piety, but for drinking, fighting and even the odd murder. Their days were numbered however, for in the

Fillongley Church, home to Maxstoke's displaced ghostly monks.

Kenilworth Castle still carries memories from the past.

1530s Henry VIII dissolved the monasteries and the monks were cast out. So any monks who came with the altar stone one would assume were already dead at that time.

There is an alternative to the church being haunted by monks from Maxstoke, for Catholic priests who served chapels and churches before the Dissolution often wore clothes very similar to monks.

The monks are not the only ones to haunt the village, for a local couple say that they are also haunted by the ghost of a thirteen-year-old called Stella. Hilda Blount told the *Coventry Evening Telegraph* in 1991, 'People have slept in one room claim to have seen a girl… Others talk of lights going on or footsteps.'

The haunted castle, Kenilworth

In Meg Elizabeth Atkins' excellent book *Haunted Warwickshire* she tells the story of a local resident whom she describes as 'Mrs Smith'. The lady in question was attending a Parent Teacher Association event at the gatehouse of the castle. She watched a group of folk musicians as they played in the oriel window which overlooks the base court.

As she was watching the singers she was suddenly aware for a few moments of a number of individuals who appeared between the musicians. One a woman was sitting sewing, wearing a plain headdress and long pale robe. Mrs Smith was struck by the woman's 'dignity and quiet happiness' but she wasn't afraid, more shaken at what she saw and the realisation that it appeared that among the company yet only she appeared to see it.

Other strange things happen around the site of the nearby Kenilworth Priory. The priory was founded in 1129 and in the sixteenth century it like all other religious houses were dissolved by Henry VIII. The last abbot was pensioned off and the house demolished and left in ruins. That, one would think, was the end of that, but despite the fact that the monks left nearly 500 years ago, some choose to remain.

It has been said that a cowled monk has been seen in Abbey Fields gliding along the avenue that leads to St Nicholas' Church. Meg Atkins says in 1978 Mr and Mrs Graham lived in Redfern Avenue. Valerie Graham began to get woken up in the early hours of the morning by the sound of chanting monks.

This state of affairs continued and on many occasions she lay in bed or stood at the window listening to the calming sound of monks chanting. She discovered that it could only be heard at the back of the house. Valerie could never share the experience with her husband for he was a heavy sleeper. Then for the first time she heard the chanting during the daytime. She called her husband, but he could hear nothing. She however continued to hear the chanting in the daytime but husband Tony to her bemusement could not and she had no proof that she wasn't imagining the reoccurring event.

After a few months the chanting stopped and Valerie gradually put it behind her. A year later her claims were backed up when she discovered that another couple about half a mile away had also heard the sound of Kenilworth's chanting monks.

Other local titles published by The History Press

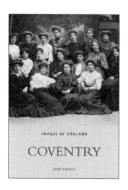

Coventry

GEOFF BARWICK

Once a medieval walled city, Coventry has thrived as home to a variety of industries, from the weaving and dying of cloth and silks which originally caused the city to prosper, through to watchmaking in the eighteenth century and the boom in the construction of motor cars in the twentieth century. This fascinating volume of over 200 photographs and illustrations offers a unique glimpse into the history of Coventry over the past 150 years.

978 0 7524 3533 6

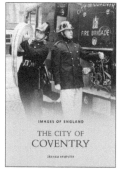

The City of Coventry

GRAHAM KEMPSTER

This collection of 170 archive photographs is drawn from the archives of the *Coventry Evening Telegraph*; the local daily newspaper which has served the people of Coventry since 1891. They highlight some of the important events that have occurred in the city during the last century, including blitz bombing during the Second World War, and the arrival of the railway at the end of the nineteenth century.

978 0 7524 3357 8

Ghost-Hunter's Casebook: The Investigations of Andrew Green Revisited

Andrew Green was one of Britain's best-known ghost hunters: *The Daily Telegraph* famously christened him 'the spectre inspector'. He investigated hundreds of hauntings during his career, and all the most intriguing cases from his lifetime of research have been collected here – updated and re-investigated by Bowen Pearse, who knew Andrew for many years. This is an essential guide for anyone with an interest in the supernatural.

978 0 7524 4500 7

Haunted Birmingham

ARTHUR SMITH AND RACHEL BANNISTER

Journey through the darker side of Birmingham: from creepy accounts of phantoms in the theatre to haunted pubs and hospitals, *Haunted Birmingham* contains a chilling range of ghostly phenomena. Drawing on historical and contemporary sources, you will hear about the landlady who haunts the site of her death, the two workmen who died during the building of the Town Hall, the late Mayor who still watches over the city, the last man to be publicly hanged in Birmingham, and many more ghostly goings on.

978 07524 4017 0

If you are interested in purchasing other books published by The History Press, or in case you have difficulty finding any of our books in your local bookshop, you can also place orders directly through our website
www.thehistorypress.co.uk